# Tips for the Dyslexic Adult.

Edited by Eorann Lean.

Published by
**The British Dyslexia Association**
Unit 8 Bracknell Beeches, Old Bracknell Lane, Bracknell, RG12 7BW

Helpline: 0845-251-9002
Administration: 0845-251-9003
Website: **www.bdadyslexia.org.uk**

Cover design and illustrations by Dianne Giblin
**www.diannegiblin.wordpress.com**
Enquiries for Dianne Giblin can be made via **admin@bdadyslexia.org.uk**

D1426102

ISBN 978-1-872653-57-0

9  781872 653570

## Editorial Note

The views expressed in this book are those of the individual contributors, and do not necessarily represent the policy of the British Dyslexia Association.

The B.D.A. does not endorse the advertisements included in this publication.

Whilst every effort has been made to ensure the accuracy of information given in this handbook, the B.D.A. cannot accept responsibility for the consequences of any errors or omissions in that information.

In certain articles the masculine pronoun is used purely for the sake of convenience.

British Dyslexia Association

978-1-872653-57-0

Published in Great Britain 2012 Copyright © British Dyslexia Association 2012

Printed by Berforts Information Press Ltd, Oxford, UK
**www.informationpress.com**

Advertising sales by Space Marketing
Tel: 01892-677-740
Fax: 01892-677-743
Email: **brians@spacemarketing.co.uk**

## British Dyslexia Association

Unit 8, Bracknell Beeches, Old Bracknell Lane, Bracknell RG12 7BW

Helpline: 0845-251-9002
Administration: 0845-251-9003
Fax: 0845-251-9005
Website: **www.bdadyslexia.org.uk**

B.D.A. is a company limited by guarantee, registered in England No. 1830587

Registered Charity No. 289243

# Foreword.

## Dr Kate Saunders.

It took me 3 years to say the words "I am Dyslexic" out loud to another human being. I was diagnosed at around 20, in my first year at university. I had struggled to get into university, retaking some A Levels. At school I had 'remedial' lessons for spelling, but up to A Level I had done quite well academically. My spelling was not always technically correct, admittedly. My English teacher told my mother at a parents evening "In all my 30 years of teaching, I have never seen anything like her spelling!" My mother, also an English teacher, agreed that neither had she, and assured him it wasn't that it hadn't been taught properly in primary school!

But I was extraordinarily lucky, my first year tutor at university (I went to study Human Psychology) was Dr. Margaret Newton, author of the Aston Index an early dyslexia screening tool for teachers, and a pioneer in dyslexia in the UK. Dr Newton was an amazing, inspirational person. She suggested I should have an assessment after seeing my handwriting on my first essay submission.

When she had carried out the assessment, she told me clearly I was intelligent and dyslexic. She explained what dyslexia is and then taught me effective study skills. I doubt that I would have passed my first year exams without these. She helped calm my anxiety that, perhaps, I was not clever enough to be at university, by assuring me that I was.

But more than this, she said the most amazing thing to me. She said "We need you to work in this field because your brain works differently, and you will see connections that we cannot. "Wow! What a turn around! She took what was a problem and a barrier and transformed it into a potential strength. She conveyed a sense of self-respect around this difference in brain functioning, and even a possible sense of social responsibility to use this difference for the good of humanity.

Thirty or so years later, I remain captivated by this view of dyslexia. I spent many years working as a specialist teacher and psychologist, assessing and teaching dyslexic individuals. The privilege of teaching dyslexic individuals is in that moment where they describe their strengths, and you stand back in awe. Don't get me wrong, I'm not saying that all dyslexics are geniuses. Only that, I have yet to meet a dyslexic who didn't have ways of learning that work for them.

This can include strengths in areas such as picture memory, three dimensional (3D) thinking skills, seeing the 'gestalt' or whole of a problem/situation, video memory (where they can 'play back that video' of what they have seen), tactile/kinaesthetic memory, memory for locus (eg. of being in a particular place and seeing it clearly in recollection) or aspects of auditory memory (eg. for mnemonics, accents). Dyslexic individuals are also generally very good at remembering stories, logic, humour and anything that makes sense. It is working with, and recalling, serial symbolic material (eg. strings of letters, numbers, unconnected instructions) and phonological skills (ie breaking down and manipulating the sounds in words) that they can struggle with.

Dyslexia is a paradox, a puzzle to the individual and those around them. The effects of dyslexia can cause tremendous frustration and impact on many areas of life.

Being dyslexic is hard work, for children and adults, it generally involves working much harder than peers in order to achieve the same results. The support and understanding of those around them is vital.

This book, 'Tips for Adult Dyslexics', is a bridge from some adult dyslexics reaching out to others. It is a book which provides useful, practised information about what dyslexia is, what support is available and, crucially, tips for strategies that dyslexic adults can adopt in order to help themselves.

Finally, there is a call to action. A plea that readers will get involved to whatever extent they can manage – whether it is through being open with others about their dyslexia and so helping to change perceptions towards dyslexia, or participating more actively in the dyslexia field. Either way, I hope the following extract from Maryanne Williamson, (1992: 190-191), will inspire you to shine.

'Our deepest fear is not that we are inadequate. Our deepest fear is that we are powerful beyond measure. It is our light, not our darkness that most frightens us. We ask ourselves, 'Who am I to be brilliant, gorgeous, talented, fabulous?' Actually, who are you not to be? ....... Your playing small doesn't serve the world. There's nothing enlightened about shrinking so that other people won't feel insecure around you. We were all meant to shine, as children do..... And as we let our light shine, we unconsciously give other people permission to do the same. As we're liberated from our own fear, our presence automatically liberates others'.

# Contents.

# Chapter 1 – Introduction to Dyslexia.

**Dr. David McLoughlin.**

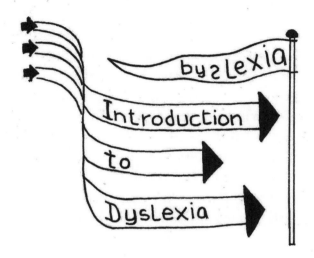

a. Dyslexia and Information processing

b. Difficulties that dyslexia can cause

c. Difficulty with transitions

d. Strengths that dyslexia can bring

e. Adult Checklist

## What is dyslexia? Its strengths and weaknesses.

## a. Dyslexia and information processing.

Dyslexic people have strengths and weakness. To understand the abilities we need to acknowledge the difficulties. Traditionally dyslexia has been regarded as a reading and spelling problem, but understanding it in this way is like thinking of chicken pox as spots. Developments in neuroscience and cognitive psychology have shown dyslexia to be an information processing problem. It is that which is inherited and persists across the lifespan. What dyslexic children and adults have in common, and what dyslexic adults have in common with their younger selves is the different way in which they process information. Problems with literacy are skill deficits that can be the result of factors such as an ineffective education.

The processing abilities involved, as well as problems that can arise when these are weak, include:

- *Phonological processing* – this underlies literacy skills, including reading and spelling

- *Rapid naming* – retrieving 'labels' quickly. It underlies skills such as reading comprehension as well as word finding, and therefore, verbal communication. It is why naming left/right can be a problem.

- *Working memory* – this is very important for effective learning and performance. It underlies 'multi-tasking', especially with words.

- *Processing speed* – the ability to process symbols quickly; it has an impact on reading and writing speed.

- *Automaticity* – the automatic development of new skills. It can take longer to acquire these.

## b. Difficulties that dyslexia can cause.

Dyslexia can present individuals with difficulties that extend beyond reading and spelling. We now refer to 'literate dyslexics'; those who can read and spell but still have other problems. It can affect everyone differently, depending on factors such as family background, educational opportunities and personality. Some of the areas that can be undermined include:

- Organisation – personal and at work
- Time management – underestimating and overestimating
- Social Communication – word finding and word order
- Writing – especially organising ideas
- Spelling – particularly in context
- Reading – often comprehension and /or speed rather than accuracy
- Maths – the procedures, including mental arithmetic and data entry

Dyslexia has been described as a 'hidden disability'. One of the advantages of this is that dyslexic people 'look normal'. This can also be a disadvantage in that the problems encountered, particularly those that extend beyond literacy, can easily be attributed to attitude and application, an individual's competencies being masked. Whereas technology can resolve many of the literacy and numeracy problems associated with dyslexia, some of the broader difficulties can be harder to resolve.

The impact can be heightened by factors such as lack of confidence, low self-esteem and anxiety. These develop as a result of the experiences dyslexic people have in learning and work settings. Not being able to forget the past can be more of a problem than being unable to remember new information. These emotional reactions can make the processing difficulties worse.

## c. Difficulty with transitions.

It is important to acknowledge that it is the transitions in life which can continue to undermine a dyslexic person's performance and highlight their difficulties. Transitions can include:

- School to further or higher education
- Education to work
- Change of job
- Promotion
- Going back to training/education
- Change of personnel

It is sometimes because dyslexic individuals have done well that their difficulties become obvious. They can be victims of their own success, particularly in a world where demands on paperwork have increased so much. Furthermore, in employment people have less control of how they use their time and deadlines are less flexible. It is at times of transition when the development of skills, as well as using alternative means of dealing with tasks such assistive technology, is especially important. Ideally people should plan and be prepared for transitions. They should be developing the skills they need now as well as for the future.

## d. Strengths that dyslexia can bring.

There are many dyslexic people working at high levels in all occupations: in business, public services, the professions, as well as design and technology. The achievements of iconic individuals have been promoted, as have those of authors, actors and architects. Many though are just hard working, conscientious and caring people who have persevered and demonstrated considerable resilience in a variety of occupational settings. They have learned very well, if differently.

The processing problems associated with dyslexia mainly occur in the left side of the brain which deals with language. Research has shown that processing in the right side which is more visual is not a problem, although the transfer of information from one side to the other can be slower. Dyslexic people are often better at using images than words, never forget a face but can't remember names. The way in which they utilise their visual abilities influences how they learn and work best.

The efficiency of the brain is determined by connections. There are high level processes such as planning, and lower order processes such as recognising words and remembering images. When connections are made between the parts that control planning and the visual components, dyslexic people can function best.

This can mean that they are big picture thinkers, can use visual planning techniques and they thrive when asked to complete portfolio work rather than take examinations. It is often why dyslexic people find their niche in the Arts and occupations such as engineering.

Information technology such as planning software, as well as text to speech and voice recognition software can provide immediate as well as long term solutions. They reduce the load on language processing and can tap visual strengths. Dyslexic people can also develop the skills and strategies they need to improve their performance. These should be task specific, suit the individual and not be too demanding. Sometimes suggested strategies are so complicated that they hinder rather than help.

**The bottom line.**

This does not mean that dyslexic people can do anything they choose to do. They need to have most of the abilities required for a course or a job. Adjustments can make up the difference, but working in a job for which one has little aptitude and taps weakness all the time only leads to anxiety and frustration. Again, therefore, it is important to acknowledge the weakness in order to capitalise on the strengths. Dealing with dyslexia can be a creative experience as it is about problem solving. Some dyslexic people become better at learning and working than others as they have given more thought to performance improvement.

## e. Adult checklist.

A checklist for dyslexic adults will not provide enough information for a diagnostic assessment, but it can be very useful in promoting a better self-understanding and a pointer towards future assessment needs.

The checklist on the next page contains the questions found to be good predictors of dyslexia (as measured by prior diagnosis). The relative importance of each question is weighted by the scores for each answer.

For each question, circle the number in the box which is closest to your response. You can keep a tally of your score as you go in the 'Total' column.

### Results from the Adults Test – what it all means.

The research and development of the checklist has provided a valuable insight into the diversity of difficulties and is a clear reminder that every individual is different and should be treated and assessed as such. However, it is also interesting to note that a number of questions, the answers to which are said to be characteristics of dyslexic adults, are commonly found in the answers of non-dyslexics.

It is important to remember that this test does not constitute an assessment of one's difficulties. It is just an indication of some of the areas in which you or the person you are assessing may have difficulties. However this questionnaire may provide a better awareness of the nature of an individual's difficulties and may indicate that further professional assessment would be helpful.

| | | Rarely | Occasionally | Often | Most of the time | Total |
|---|---|---|---|---|---|---|
| 1 | Do you confuse visually similar words such as cat and cot? | 3 | 6 | 9 | 12 | |
| 2 | Do you lose your place or miss out lines when reading? | 2 | 4 | 6 | 8 | |
| 3 | Do you confuse the names of objects, for example table for chair? | 1 | 2 | 4 | 4 | |
| 4 | Do you have trouble telling left from right? | 1 | 2 | 4 | 4 | |
| 5 | Is map reading or finding your way to a strange place confusing? | 1 | 2 | 4 | 4 | |
| 6 | Do you re-read paragraphs to understand them? | 1 | 2 | 4 | 4 | |
| 7 | Do you get confused when given several instructions at once? | 1 | 2 | 4 | 4 | |
| 8 | Do you make mistakes when taking down telephone messages? | 1 | 2 | 4 | 4 | |
| 9 | Do you find it difficult to find the right word to say? | 1 | 2 | 4 | 4 | |
| 10 | How often do you think of creative solutions to problems? | 1 | 2 | 4 | 4 | |
| | | Easy | Challenging | Difficult | Very Difficult | Total |
| 11 | How easy do you find it to sound out words such as e-le-phant? | 3 | 6 | 9 | 12 | |
| 12 | When writing, do you find it difficult to organise thoughts on paper? | 2 | 4 | 6 | 8 | |
| 13 | Did you learn your multiplication tables easily? | 2 | 4 | 6 | 8 | |
| 14 | How easy do you find it to recite the alphabet? | 1 | 2 | 3 | 4 | |
| 15 | How hard do you find it to read aloud? | 1 | 2 | 3 | 4 | |

Whilst we do stress that this is not a diagnostic tool, research suggests the following:

**Score less than 45** – probably non-dyslexic.

Research results: no individual who was diagnosed as dyslexic through a full assessment was found to have scored less than 45 and therefore it is unlikely that if you score under 45 you will be dyslexic.

**Score 45 to 60** – showing signs consistent with mild dyslexia.

Research results: most of those who were in this category showed signs of being at least moderately dyslexic. However, a number of persons not previously diagnosed as dyslexic (though they could just be unrecognised and undiagnosed) fell into this category.

**Score Greater than 60** – signs consistent with moderate or severe dyslexia.

Research results: all those who recorded scores of more than 60 were diagnosed as moderately or severely dyslexic. Therefore we would suggest that a score greater than 60 suggests moderate or severe dyslexia. Please note that this should not be regarded as an assessment of one's difficulties. But if you feel that a dyslexia-type problem may exist, further advice should be sought.

Copyright Ian Smythe and John Everatt, 2001.
This may be copied for the benefit of dyslexic adults.

For further information on dyslexia:

Read:

**Dyslexia – A Beginner's Guide** – by Nicola Brunswick.
Published by Oneworld

**The Gift of Dyslexia** – By Ronald D Davis.
Published by Souvenir Press Ltd

Go to:

**British Dyslexia Association** website:
www.bdadyslexia.org.uk

**Dyslexia Action Website**
www.dyslexiaaction.org.uk

Call:

**B.D.A. Helpline** 0845-251-9002

# Chapter 2 – Assessments.

**Dr Sylvia Moody.**

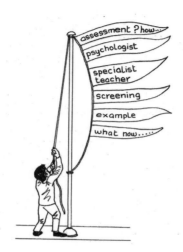

a. Could you be dyslexic?

b. Could you have associated difficulties? e.g., dyspraxia, attentin deficit disorder, visual processing problems

c. How can you arrange a diagnostic assessment?

d. Who pays for the diagnostic assessment?

e. What happens in a diagnostic assessment?

f. What happens after a diagnostic assessment?

g. What might you feel after a diagnostic assessment?

h. How can you arrange a workplace needs assessment?

i. How can you check the credentials of the workplace needs assessor?

j. What should you expect in a workplace needs assessment?

k. What should your workplace needs report tell you?

## Diagnostic and needs assessments.

### a. Could you be dyslexic?

If you suspect that you might have dyslexic difficulties, and are wondering if an assessment would be useful, the first thing to do is to write down a list of all the difficulties you feel you are experiencing.

Don't confine yourself just to difficulties with literacy skills; consider also whether you might have difficulties with listening skills, speaking succinctly, memory, organisational skills, dealing with sequences, (such as the months of the year), or performing tasks that require you to create a structure of some kind, be it structuring a piece of written work, your time, your work schedule or just daily life.

Then write down a few things that you think you can do well: perhaps you are quick-thinking, creative, have an entrepreneurial flair, good people skills, good IT or technological abilities.

It is a particular pattern of strengths and weaknesses that characterises specific learning difficulties (or differences) such as dyslexia.

### b. Could you have associated difficulties, e.g., dyspraxia, attention deficit disorder, visual processing problems?

You may feel that you have a pattern of difficulties which looks something like the list in the previous section but not quite – perhaps your reading is quite good but you have difficulties with writing, organisational skills and social skills. Perhaps you are clumsy and often knock things over or trip up. If so, then it may be that your difficulties are *dyspraxic* in nature. (Some people have both dyslexic and dyspraxic difficulties together.)

Again, if you feel that your main problems are an inability to concentrate and focus on tasks, if you are constantly restless both physically and mentally, if you are impulsive, sometimes reckless, and prone to mood swings, then you could consider whether you have *attention deficit disorder*.

Finally, if you have some difficulties in looking at print, for example if you see lines of print moving about and find white paper 'glaring' (all of which can occur with people who either already have glasses or don't need glasses), then it is possible that you have some subtle *visual processing problems* – perhaps visual stress. This means your brain gets confused by complex patterns, or binocular problems, and that your eyes are a bit lazy about focussing together.

Every person is different. Some people will have all of the above types of difficulty; others may have no more than one, and many people are in between the two extremes.

Before thinking about arranging an assessment, it is wise to inform yourself more about whichever of the above conditions you suspect you may have.

## c. How can you arrange a diagnostic assessment?

The best way to find an assessor is through the help organisations listed at the end of this book. According to which difficulties you think you have, it is very important to check that any assessor you contact is competent to assess for your particular pattern of difficulties. Some assessors confine themselves to dyslexia, others to dyslexia and dyspraxia and so on.

Don't hesitate to ask the assessor about their specific area of expertise; if you find it difficult to do this over the telephone, then email the assessor listing the difficulties you think you have and asking if the assessor is able to cover them.

## d. Who pays for the diagnostic assessment?

If you are a student, it is possible that your institution may recommend an assessor and fund your diagnostic assessment in whole or in part. If you are in the workplace you may have to find the assessor yourself but some employers may be willing to pay for the assessment.

Please note in particular that it would almost certainly be inappropriate for you to be referred (for instance by your firm's occupational health adviser) to the NHS for an assessment. This is because psychologists in the health service usually specialise in seeing either children with developmental difficulties or adults who have acquired dyslexia (e.g. as a result of stroke or head injury); such psychologists do not usually have the relevant expertise or tests to assess developmental adult dyslexia.

## e. What happens in a diagnostic assessment?

The assessor (eg a suitably qualified psychologist or dyslexia specialist teacher / assessor) will begin by talking with you to get a good idea about your general background and the sort of strengths, difficulties and coping strategies you feel you have. He/she will administer relevant checklists and you will be asked to do a variety of tests, e.g. of perception, memory, reading.

It is important to stress that the tests you do are not of a pass/fail type – the assessor is not interested in how well you do but simply *how* you do, i.e. what are your strengths and weaknesses. Different patterns of strengths and weaknesses indicate different types of specific learning difficulty. The assessor will explain what he/she has found at the end of the assessment and provide you in due course with a detailed report.

According to the findings of the assessment you may be referred on to a dyslexia tutor, a dyspraxia specialist, an ADHD specialist, or some combination of the above, to learn strategies and skills that will be useful to you.

You may also be referred on to an optometrist, if you have visual processing difficulties; an occupational therapist, if you have severe difficulties with movement; a speech and language therapist, if you have difficulties with articulating words or forming grammatical sentences; and to a counsellor or therapist if you have emotional problems.

## f. What happens after an assessment?

If you are a student, you should be referred on by your institution for a *study needs assessment* to find out precisely what help would be useful to you. This assessment and any support you are deemed to need would be funded by the student's respective funder. These include Students Awards Agency for Scotland, for Scottish students; Student Finance Wales, for Welsh students; Northern Ireland Finance, for Northern Irish students and Student Finance England, for English students.

If you are in the workplace, you or your employer will need to arrange a *workplace needs assessment* (see section h. below).

## g. What might you feel after a diagnostic assessment?

If, before the assessment, you had already felt pretty sure you had some type of dyslexic difficulties, then you will probably simply feel relieved to have your suspicions confirmed and to be able to move on to getting some appropriate help.

If you had been unsure that you had dyslexic or associated difficulties, or if you had never even suspected that you might have such difficulties, a 'diagnosis of dyslexia' might leave you with mixed feelings: relief that your problems had been identified and that help would be provided, but also sadness, even anger, that the difficulties had not been identified previously.

The oldest client I have seen was aged 74 years – she had finally realised that she was dyslexic when she decided to study for a degree at the Open University. It's not hard to see that in such a case the immense relief she felt about finally being able to understand herself was mingled with painful grief for a life which she felt had in many ways been lost.

Obviously the older a person is when they finally come
to understand the nature of their problems, the more
difficult initially is the adjustment to the new situation.
A period of grieving for what might seem lost years is
quite natural and indeed healthy, and most people in this
situation find that they eventually start to look forward
rather than back and that they become determined
to make the most of the life still ahead of them.

## h. How can you arrange a workplace needs assessment?

There are two ways of arranging a workplace needs
assessment, each of which has advantages and
disadvantages.

The first way is to arrange the assessment through the
government's *Access to Work* scheme. The advantage
of this route is that Access to Work will pay for the
assessment. Disadvantages are that your assessment
may not always be carried out by a dyslexia/dyspraxia
specialist, a skills training programme may not
be specified, and your employer may not receive
advice about reasonable adjustments. (For more
information on Access to Work see chapter 3)

The second route is to go through a *private dyslexia
organisation* which specialises in carrying out workplace
needs assessments and in writing reports in a form
acceptable to Access to Work. If you do approach a private
organisation (or practitioner) to get a needs assessment,
it is essential to check that they are qualified to offer this

service. Your local British Dyslexia Association branch should be able to help you find a suitable assessor.

The disadvantage of the private route is that you, or your employer, will have to fund the assessment. Advantages are that the assessment will be carried out by a dyslexia/dyspraxia expert, who will be able to specify a detailed skills training programme (a crucial element in the support package), recommend IT support, and advise your employer on reasonable adjustments and legal obligations.

Whichever route you go on for the *assessment*, you can still apply to Access to Work for *funding for the training or equipment* you require.

## i. How can you check the credentials of the assessor?

When arranging a workplace needs assessment you (or your employer) need to establish that the assessor is experienced in *workplace consultancy* and will be able to recommend *a workplace skills training programme* as well as IT support. Below are some suggested specific questions that you could email to the assessor:

- What proportion of your practice is given to workplace dyslexia consultancy?
- Can you produce a workplace needs report acceptable to Access to Work?
- Will your report contain recommendations for workplace skills training as well as IT recommendations?

- Can you advise my employer on reasonable adjustments in the workplace and related legal issues?

## j. What should you expect in a workplace needs assessment?

In a workplace needs assessment, you will not be asked to do any tests. Rather, the assessor will ask you in detail about the nature and demands of your job, the strengths you bring to it, the difficulties you have with it, the coping strategies you use, and the support given (or not) by your employer. He/she will subsequently contact your employer to discuss reasonable adjustments which the latter could make in order to help and support you at work.

## k. What should your workplace needs report tell you?

Your assessment report should include recommendations for *all* of the following:

- A detailed workplace skills training programme which covers all aspects of literacy which are directly related to your work – for instance, form filling, data entry, research skills, report writing, reading quickly with good comprehension.

- General work skills should also be covered, e.g., dealing with job interviews or work reviews, contributing to meetings, understanding instructions, time management, organisational skills.

- An initial training programme should ideally be around 30 hours spread over a period of at least three months (however government funded programmes rarely provide this much). The name of a recommended trainer should be given.

- IT recommendations including advice on how the IT training should be carried out.

It is not useful for training to be delivered in just one day, or one half-day; rather it should be spread out over several short sessions. The trainer should be knowledgeable about dyslexia (and associated conditions) and deliver the training in a manner and at a pace suitable for the trainee. The name of a recommended trainer should be given.

- Detailed recommendations to the employer about reasonable adjustments, i.e. what actions the employer can take to support the training programme – for example, giving time off for training, providing a quiet workspace, allowing extra time for tasks to be completed. A note should also be included about the legal obligations of employers towards employees with specific learning difficulties.

If the report you receive does not include *all* of the above sections, you should take up the matter with the assessor, or with the organisation that has provided the assessor, and request relevant additions to the recommendations, and even a further assessment, if necessary. It is important to stress this point, because it frequently happens that dyslexic employees, after going through the long process of diagnostic and needs assessments, do not receive a comprehensive training package. Adequate training can make all the difference between keeping and losing a job.

To find more information:

## Go To:

**British Dyslexia association** – information on Dyslexia – **www.bdadyslexia.org.uk**

**DANDA** – information on Dyspraxia – **www.danda.org.uk**

**AADD–UK** – information on Attendtion Defecit (hyperactivity) Disorder – **www.aadduk.org**

**Institute of Colorimetry** – information on visual stress – **www.colorimetryinstitute.org**

**PATOSS** – General information on all of the above: **www.patoss-dyslexia.org**

**Working With Dyslexia** – Videos on what it's like to have an assessment – **www.workingwithdyslexia.com**

## Read:

Dyslexia: How to Survive and Succeed at Work. By Sylvia Moody. Random House (Vermilion).

Living with Dyspraxia. By Mary Colley. Jessica Kingsley.

That's the way I think: dyslexia and dyspraxia explained. By David Grant. David Fulton

## Books:

For ADHD:

Delivered from Distraction. By Edward Hallowell and Luke Ratey. Simon and Schuster.

ADD – friendly ways to Organise your Life. By Judith Kolberg and Kathleen Nadeau. Routledge.

## Call:

The British Dyslexia Association's helpline –list of specialist tutor dyslexia assessors and advice 0845 251 9002

**Patoss** – for list of specialist tutor dyslexia assessors: 01386 712 650

**Access to Work** – to arrange a workplace assessment: 020 8426 3110

## Patoss - The largest professional association for SpLD Specialist Teachers in the UK

Membership of Patoss includes not only Specialist Teachers but is also open to other individuals and organisations with an interest in the field of specific learning difficulties.

- Patoss is the largest provider of SpLD Assessment Practicing Certificates.
- Patoss supplies a National Index of Tutors and Assessors of SpLD.
- Patoss offers an ongoing CPD programme and provides bespoke in house training for a range of organisations.

**Further information about Patoss is available at www.patoss-dyslexia.org or phone 01386 712650, or email patoss@sworcs.ac.uk**

## We can provide solutions to help you **achieve your potential** at Work, School, or University..

**Assistive software** for your computer, at work or in your educational establishment, such as voice recognition, screen readers and mind mapping, can all help with the use of your computer.

**Hardware accessories** such as reading pens, hand held spell checkers, dictaphones and overlays can help to increase productivity.

**Ergonomic assessments** and **solutions** to ensure your workspace is right for you.

**Contact Wyvern today to see how we can help you..**

## www.wbs.uk.com/bda
## 01432 271233

# Chapter 3 – Employment.

a. Choosing a Career

b. How dyslexia might affect you at work and coping strategies

c. Should I tell my employer? How will this help?

d. Dyslexia and Disability discrimination at work

e. What is an employment tribunal like?

f. Self-Employment and entrepreneurism

g. Personal Experience: setting up your own business

# a. Choosing a career.

### Brian Hagan.

I am often asked – 'Are certain career paths and specific jobs well suited – or not suited – to dyslexic employees'?

Given the unique needs of each dyslexic job applicant, rather than recommending certain careers, I prefer to outline a process that helps maximise their chances of:

> a) Choosing the right career path and securing a post.
>
> b) Avoiding the wrong career path.

This careers selection process is based on 20 years senior experience in Human Resources and 12 subsequent years integrating this experience within my second career as a qualified dyslexia tutor, assessor and mentor.

I hope it will help you work systematically through a number of logical stages, and choose a career which will: –

> • Capitalise on your strengths and motivation, AND
>
> • Address or avoid areas of weakness.

### Stage 1. Appraisal of Careers Options.

1. To begin to analyse what career direction might best suit your strengths and motivations, you should start by:

> • Reflecting on your general strengths and less strong areas – use the Gibbs model (please see further information box).

- Analysing your diagnostic assessment, and any other reports produced post 16 e.g. FE/HE and workplace assessments. Most assessors will be happy – given a little notice, to expand on their reports for you.

- Combine this information and check out how your skills match career profiles on career websites (please see further information box).

- Find links to other sites that will help you explore your options and help you begin to make some preliminary decisions (please see further information box).

- Other publications like The Guardian Careers Guide, and The Penguin Careers Guide are also very helpful in exploring career paths you may not have heard of, or want to know more about.

- You can use these resources to generate career options by:

- Identifying your career niches; that is, the occupational areas that motivate you most

- Generating options by matching these career niches to the job requirements – job description and person specification – for your favourite careers.

## Stage 2. Matching your strengths to job requirements.

Stage 1 is vital in helping you reduce the career market to more manageable proportions – the process should help you create a shortlist of potentially desirable career paths, and the websites and books will have detailed information on salaries, application procedures and what the careers are about.

Stage 2 is equally important in helping you ensure that the job demands are at a level where you are confident that you can perform effectively after induction.

**To decide this you need to:**

- Exclude those job choices where there is a significant gap between the job requirements and your pattern of strengths and less strong areas.
- Prioritise the remaining options.
- Draw up an action plan to apply for jobs drawn from your prioritised options.

**You can do this by:**

- Systematically recording your strengths and weaknesses (using your diagnostic assessment).
- Comparing these to the job description of the posts you wish to apply for.
- Analysing what proportion of the job requires knowledge skills and experience that you have been able to demonstrate consistently and those you have not got.

If you are proficient in more than 85–90 per cent of the key job requirements **add the job to your career shortlist.**

If however you are proficient in less than 80 per cent and cannot readily bridge these gaps through training to improve your skills – in say assistive technology or business – **then you should avoid the job**!

Don't be tempted to take badly matched jobs and hope you'll be ok – sadly my experience is that dyslexia unaware employers mistake common features of dyslexia for lack of attention to detail, or laziness, and end up discriminating against otherwise motivated and hardworking dyslexic employees.

Avoiding the stress and discrimination the wrong career choice can bring is vital.

Exploring realistically what you can and can't do now – and after training in dyslexia related skills – will pay dividends in the medium term.

Whilst recognising and accepting that everyone has fears about disclosure, I always recommend it. It gives the opportunity to present the hard work, additional skills and determination you will have shown to overcome your dyslexic difficulties.

And remember, employers have a legal duty to make reasonable adjustments for potential as well as existing employees – you should analyse the selection process and make suggestions that will help you display your full range of competencies during the selection process.

## Stage 3. Putting Your Career Plan into Action.

Putting the plan into action involves ensuring that you have a careers adviser who has a professional understanding of dyslexia, as well as experience in helping clients locate, apply for and secure suitable jobs, based on assessing the candidate's knowledge, skills, motivation and experience.

However the quality and effectiveness of careers advice to dyslexic clients provided by the agencies involved is often less expert than it needs to be.

You should therefore insist that those providing careers advice are able to fully understand the detailed information in your diagnostic and other assessments.

They must also ensure that their advice on future career development is integrated with, and based on a full understanding of your strengths and less strong areas, and the practical workplace implications of this for their recommended career choices.

You should also expect an effective careers adviser to support you to produce an overall timed career search plan which:-

- Sets out how to find dyslexia-friendly employers and get further information on specific careers with them.

- Sets objectives for your career search e.g. making four targeted requests each week for suitable job descriptions and person specifications from dyslexia friendly employers.

- Sets out information to support job applications, including preparing an effective CV, which addresses issues of disclosure and practising interview techniques.

- Suggests resources relevant to the plan, e.g. careers websites, government support and helpful publication.

I am happy to discuss the issues outlined in this article further with interested readers.

For more information:

**British Dyslexia Association website** – Disability Discrimination information and rights

**http://www.bdadyslexia.org.uk/ about-dyslexia/adults-and-business/ disability-discrimination-act-.html**

**The National Careers Service** – national careers information and advice

**www.nationalcareersservice.direct.gov.uk**

**The Gibbs Cycle** – to help with reflection on career strengths **www2.hud.ac.uk/hhs/staffsupport/ lqsu_files/Gibbs_Reflective_Cycle.pdf**

**Palgrave Study Skills** – provides information and suggest resources for personal development and career choice

**www.palgrave.com/skills4study/pdp/useful/index.asp**

**Disability Job Site** – provides guidance and job searches

**www.disabilityjobsite.co.uk**

Contact the author:

**Brian Hagan** – Dyslexia Advice & Training Services

**bhdyslexia@yahoo.co.uk**

## b. How dyslexia might affect you at work and coping strategies.
### Sharon Blake.

Today's ever changing work environment puts greater demands than ever on our skills and strengths. We now operate in a fast paced, technology driven and knowledge based work space where increasingly we are required to achieve.

For adults with dyslexia, those challenges become amplified and often lead to increased levels of anxiety. Regaining the feeling of control over certain areas of your work can have the effect of reducing your levels of concern, helping you to cope with the daily work demands more effectively.

You may already have well developed coping strategies that you have refined over time or have learnt from other sources. For example, writing things down, task swapping with colleagues or using assistive functions on your phone.

In this article you will find suggestions on how dyslexia might affect you at work, along with some useful, trustworthy strategies and mechanisms to make your work life just that little bit easier.

Adults with dyslexia frequently report that they encounter the following;-

1. Issues with working memory
2. Challenges around sequencing and processes
3. Difficulties with organisation and time planning

The aim of this article is to provide you with some simple and straightforward tips around these 3 areas, which you can apply straight away.

**Issues with working memory.**

Do you ever find yourself struggling to recall messages? Perhaps you miss the thread of a conversation in a meeting? Maybe you lose track part way through a job you are doing?

Working memory is used for information that needs to be temporarily stored before it moves to your stronger long term memory. For example; capturing a telephone number or remembering someone's name during a brief conversation.

To assist your working memory to cope with all the information coming at you on a daily basis, try the following;-

- Chunk information down, often 2-3 items works well for adults with dyslexia so aim to recall 2-3 key things, chunk telephone numbers into blocks of 2-3 or consider what 2-3 key bullet points you want to communicate in your emails.

- Know what your preferred learning style is. We tend to learn through visual (what we see), auditory (what we hear or are told) and kinaesthetic (what we feel or demonstrate) modes. By using your strongest preferences, you can assist your weaker areas.

- Explore and incorporate concept mapping techniques; these can greatly assist working memory as some dyslexic brains seem to naturally lean towards lateral, creative, random, pictures and patterns.

- Learning and understanding skimming and scanning methods may help you to better absorb written documents, whereby the key works and messages are highlighted in the document. The aim of this is get the overall content and essence of the material rather than reading and re-reading it word for word.

Here is what a concept map might look like, although you will have your own way of creating your own version;-

**Challenges around sequencing and processes.**

How often do you find that you miss out aspects of your work or skip important stages? Perhaps you find alphabetical filing confusing?

So much of our daily working life revolves around processes, procedures, sequences and order. As you may have experienced, this can pose difficulties for dyslexic adults.

Try the following to help you;-

- Create flow charts to guide you through process and procedures so that you have all the information in one visible diagram which you can refer to as you need it.

- Use templates or checklists to ensure you cover all necessary areas, this will save you from having to commit this to your memory.

- Think about what memory aids can help you with processes you don't need to complete on a regular basis.

An example of a simple flowchart is opposite;-

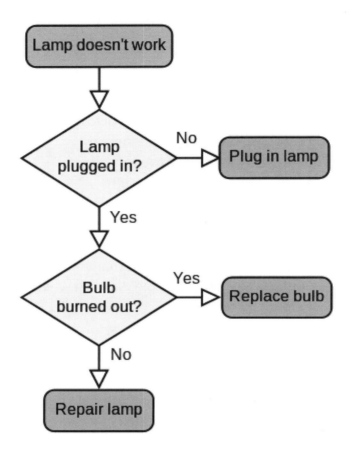

**Difficulties with organisation and time planning.**

Do you often find that time just seems to slip out from under you? Maybe you struggle to find important papers, e-mails or folders? Do colleagues give you feedback that you appear disorganised?

- Identify your most effective periods for working so that you can organise your most demanding tasks into that time, do you work best in the morning when you are fresh or do you prefer the afternoon shift?

- Consider colour coding your to do list like traffic lights: red for the biggest priority, amber for less urgent/important and green for least important/urgent.

- Create regular to do lists and review them regularly, taking time at the beginning and end of each day to check what you have completed and the tasks still outstanding.

By using some of the practical and straightforward suggestions made in this article, you will notice that you save time, effort and energy whilst feeling more productive and happier during your working day. Well, hopefully most of the time!

For more information:

Read:

**Dyslexia in the Workplace** – by Margaret Malpas. Published by British Dyslexia Association

**Dyslexia: How to Survive and Succeed at Work** – By Sylvia Moody. Published by Random House (Vermilion).

**Supporting Dyslexic Adults in Higher education and Employment** – edited by Nicola Brunswick. Published by Wiley-Blackwell

Call:

**B.D.A. helpline** – for list of tutors who can help with coping strategies

Contact the author:

**Sharon Blake** – Trainer for dyslexia coping strategies.

**sharonblake2@gmail.com**

## c. Should I tell my employer? How will this help?
**Janette Beetham.**

Whether an employee should inform their employer about a Specific Learning Difficulty or not should be a simple and straight forward question to answer – 'yes'. However, due to the lack of comprehensive understanding of dyslexia across the employment sphere and the tendency for dyslexic people not to want to draw attention to their learning difference, the answer to this first question is extremely subjective.

Many dyslexic people describe themselves as always feeling they have had to work harder than their peers – simply to keep up. Thus for many sheer determination and hard work tend to be part of their recipe for success. However, with this often also comes poor self-concept and confidence issues. Therefore talking about any challenges and needing help does not sit easily. The problems they are having may be stressful, but the thought of disclosure can be the cause of extreme anxiety.

Sadly, this means that often in cases where dyslexic employees are experiencing challenges, the first time dyslexia is openly discussed is when formal performance procedures have been actioned.

However, employers have a legal obligation to provide reasonable adjustments under the Equality Act 2010. This means that individuals should have specialist help available to them. Telling your employer means that you can receive this help (that is a right and not a privilege) and avoid the misunderstandings that lead to formal procedures.

WHEN ABILITY AND PERFORMANCE JUST DON'T SEEM TO MATCH... dyslexia think

©Janette Beetham 2012

It is now becoming more widely recognised that an 'accessible' workplace, particularly a dyslexia friendly one, makes good business sense. It can be a more effective and productive work environment with both internal and external communications. This means that a dyslexia disclosure should be received with better understanding. Many organisations will have a set process that works best for them linked to their current Disability Policy. Of course, employers may not have had a declared dyslexic employer before and may only be at the beginning of their dyslexia ‹journey›. In these cases it is important to approach disclosure with confidence and clarity to help employers› to understand. You will need to point out the strengths that your dyslexia gives you alongside your needs. For instance ‹ My dyslexia effects my short term memory which means that I have become very good at being organised, keeping written notes and check-lists. What I would like is some software/support to help me manage this even better.›

Having a good rapport with a line manager can make it much easier to discuss any work related challenges & concerns. Therefore working on your relationship with your manager and having regular appraisals/catch-up meetings can help you to feel ‹safe› with them before disclosing your dyslexia. If there is someone else within management or HR that you enjoy a good relationship with then this may be the best person to talk to first. The manager would most probably then liaise with Human Resources and the individual would be guided according to the organisation's Dyslexia Policy or established process.

Telling your employer does not only avoid misunderstandings but can lead to support you deserve. The type of support will vary according the needs of the individual but would most likely be one of these:

- One to One Coping Strategies Coaching
- One to One Literacy/Numeracy Tutoring
- Workplace Needs Assessment
- Application to Access to Work

The first step will normally be to get a Workplaces Needs Assessment in order to get a full documented report on your needs and recommended support. Both of these options would be arranged and paid for by the employer. (An employer that has previous experience of dyslexia may simply arrange for the individual to have a series of coping strategies coaching with specialist)

**Access to Work.**

A Work Place Assessment will normally take place through the government's scheme Access to Work. This application is made by the dyslexic individual and it is not necessary for you to have a full diagnostic assessment to apply to Access to Work for a Workplace Needs Assessment.

It is advisable to talk to someone at work prior to making an application. This is because Workplace Needs Assessor will normally have to come 'on site' for the assessment meeting and the employer will be expected to pay for the costs of any recommended support. (Dependent upon the size of the business the employer may be able to claim some or all of the costs back from Access to work – see below for more info).

---

How much will the employer have to pay under the Access to Work scheme?

"The precise level of cost sharing is determined as follows:

- Employers with 1 to 9 employees will not be expected share costs.

- Employers with 10 to 49 employees will pay the first £300 and 20% of costs up to £10,000.

- Employers with 50 to 249 employees will pay the first £500 and 20% of costs up to £10,000.

- Large employers with 250 or more employees will pay the first £1,000 and 20% of costs up to £10,000" (DWP, 2012).

NB. In addition to the criteria for reimbursement there is also a review undertaken concerning business benefit which may reduce the amount of funding allowed by Department for Work & Pensions.

---

An early disclosure to your employer means that you can receive the help you deserve from Access to Work at the beginning rather than once you're struggling. It also helps out your employer as if an Access to

Work Workplace Assessment application is actioned within 6 weeks of starting a new job the Assessment and the costs of the resulting recommendations for reasonable adjustments may be covered in full by Access to Work. (Dependent upon individual eligibility).

Attitudes towards dyslexia and specific learning difficulties vary depending upon the level of awareness within the organisation, the corporate culture, procedures and the awareness and personal experience of line managers and supervisors.

Consequently, each individual dyslexic will need to make decisions on how best to approach their own employer. Doing some initial ground work on how the organisation has worked with dyslexic employees in recent times should help to ensure you approach any future dyslexia focused conversations in the way you feel you will get the best outcome.

---

For more information:

For Workplace Needs Assessments and other assessments go to Chapter 2 in this book.

**Go to:**

**Access to Work** – The Government's scheme for workplace assessments.

**www.direct.gov.uk/accesstowork**

## d. Dyslexia and disability discrimination in the workplace.

**John Mackenzie.**

Dyslexia and related Specific Learning Difficulties are disabilities covered by the **Equality Act 2010,** which replaces the Disability Discrimination Act 1995.

All organisations, except the Armed Forces, are required to ensure that people with disabilities are not treated unfavourably and are offered reasonable adjustments. Originally intended to combat discrimination in the workplace, the Equality Act now covers education, suppliers of goods and services, public bodies and local authorities.

Since 2005, **The Disability Equality Duty** has highlighted anti-discriminatory practices, requiring all public bodies to adopt a proactive approach to incorporating disability equality into all decisions and activities, encapsulated in a Disability Equality Scheme and reviewed under regular Equality Impact Assessments. To date, this process has focused on physical disabilities and mental illness, and has tended to neglect the needs of the large population with Specific Learning Difficulties.

A disabled person is defined by the Equality Act as one who has a long standing condition that has an adverse effect on his or her ability to perform day-to-day tasks. As dyslexia is a life-long condition, provided it is sufficiently significant, an employee with dyslexic difficulties is disabled under the Act.

The condition needs only to be 'more than trivial' to be disabling. In practice, where a dyslexic candidate is considered to be in need of 25% extra time in tests and exams (a very common recommendation in assessment reports that diagnose dyslexia) the individual will be considered disabled under the Act.

Reasonable adjustments are styled 'reasonable', rather than mandatory, to take into account particular circumstances. For instance a small newsagent in a listed building with a door step would not be expected to install a wheelchair ramp, but they may be expected to serve someone in a wheelchair from the door. Smaller organisations may not be in a financial position to offer the accommodations expected of large ones.

Many organisations have a long way to go to make their services dyslexia friendly, from accessible websites through to offering information in electronic format, to helping with form-filling. Many service providers have some work to do here in relation to Specific Learning Difficulties, including Jobcentres, banks and the retail sector.

In employment, an employer can receive help from the government's Access to Work scheme (see previous section), which is essentially a grant to the employee to help with the cost of implementing appropriate reasonable adjustments. A workplace needs assessment identifies and recommends the appropriate adjustments, but it is down to the employer to implement these if 'reasonable'.

In the case of dyslexia, employers can sometimes be slow to implement the recommended adjustments. Failure to make reasonable adjustments is a common finding in dyslexia Employment Tribunal cases.

**Dyslexia and Employment Law.**

- Equality Act 2010 replaces the Disability Discrimination Act 1995.

- Employers must not discriminate against a disabled person in

  - Recruitment.

  - Promotion.

  - Appraisals.

  - Training and development.

  - The dismissal process.

- Employers have a duty to implement 'reasonable adjustments' to support employees with a disability.

- The Equality Act covers:

  - Direct Discrimination (overt discrimination because someone is dyslexic).

  - Indirect Discrimination or Disability Related Discrimination (discrimination relating to the effects of dyslexia).

  - Harassment (bullying, treating someone in a demeaning way because of dyslexic difficulties).

   o  Victimisation (unfavourable treatment where an employee has complained).

## e. What is an employment tribunal like?
**John Mackenzie.**

Proceedings are conducted on the basis of written statements and documentation. Each party is cross examined by the other side, beginning with the Claimant. The Claimant's statement is therefore a critically important document.

All documentation is provided for the opposing party prior to the hearing. The most successful actions are frequently those involving failure to implement reasonable adjustments, which may often be easily demonstrated.

To prove harassment, this may be more problematic and a claimant will need to provide factual evidence (diaries, email trails, statements from colleagues, medical evidence of stress).

Similarly, claims for constructive dismissal (where employment circumstances have been made so intolerable for the employee that they leave), are much harder to prove than straightforward unfair dismissal.

Claims for discrimination in the recruitment process, such as lack of reasonable adjustments at interview, are very difficult to establish. Compensation is likely to be small and may not cover legal costs.

Settling a case before action may often be more favourable financially. The whole process of appearing before a Tribunal can be particularly stressful for the dyslexic claimant. Under professional cross examination, the dyslexic claimant may not always perform well. Contrary to popular misconception, Tribunal awards are not large.

For more information and advice:

Go to or Call:

**B.D.A. helpline** – for advice and information Tel: 0845-251-9002

**The Disability Law Service** – provides free legal advice to disabled people and representation where appropriate

Tel: 020-7791-9800 Web: **http://www.dls.org.uk**

**RADAR** – provides advice on the Act. Tel: 020-7250-3222  Web: **http://www.radar.org.uk**

Information for your employer:

**Employers Forum on Disability** – information and rescources Tel: 020-7403-3020 Web: **http://www.employers-forum.co.uk**

**B.D.A.'s code of conduct for employers** – order at the B.D.A. store **www.bdastore.org.uk**

## f. Self-employment and entrepreneurism.
### Professor Julie Logan.

Many entrepreneurs and successful self-employed people are dyslexic. In fact, there is a much higher incidence of those who are dyslexic among these groups than in the normal adult population (Logan, 2001). Are people with dyslexia forced into entrepreneurship and self-employment or do they choose this path? How can we be sure they will be successful?

**Pushed or Pulled.**

There are both negative and positive reasons for people with dyslexia choosing to become self employed.

Starting a venture may be preferable to coping with the difficulties encountered on a daily basis in the corporate environment. Despite dyslexic employees bringing desirable qualities such as creativity, people skills and entrepreneurial ability, many companies struggle to recognise and support their needs. Furthermore they are unable to control their environment (Fitzgibbon and O'Conner, 2002). In consequence the corporate workplace can be very stressful for dyslexics (Hales, 1995: Reid & Kirk, 2001).

Therefore some dyslexic adults leave the corporate environment because they believe they can succeed more easily by running their own company (Logan 2010).

On the positive side, many dyslexic people choose entrepreneurship and self-employment because it plays to their strengths which often include good communication and people skills. Successful dyslexic entrepreneurs have learned coping strategies to manage their dyslexia and utilized their strengths to give them a head start over non-dyslexic entrepreneurs. As a consequence many grow their ventures rapidly (Logan, 2009).

### What skills do dyslexic individuals have to be successful entrepreneurs?

The dyslexic entrepreneurs in Logan's (2010) study displayed highly developed skills vital for business success: communication, leadership, and delegation.

An **excellent oral communication** ability, probably developed to compensate for weaknesses in written communication, helped to gain an edge in business. The entrepreneurs had a vision for their business and were able to communicate this persuasively. They "painted pictures" to explain concepts to those around them. This is a very powerful tool; as it can help a difficult concept to be understood more readily.

> In terms of wanting to get people behind you to deliver a business, then that's about communication, that's about standing up and inspiring people, that's about telling stories, that's about painting pictures with words that people can follow so that they want to do whatever it is that needs to be done. ZA

The entrepreneurs used **great interpersonal skills** to lead and motivate by developing personal and long-lasting relationships with their team (Taylor and Walter, 2003; Logan, 2010). Throughout their lives, these entrepreneurs had been able to persuade and rely on others for help.

> I built up a great team of people around me. One of the major strengths if I look back was my ability to pick great people, to work with them and to create a wonderful environment where everyone wanted to succeed together. DR

Those who are dyslexic learn early in life to delegate in order to cope. Bringing this skill to their new venture gives them an advantage and, because they have to delegate, they value those around them.

> *Delegation is considered to be one of the most important attributes of a successful business-person. I naturally delegate; I have to delegate. There's no way I can get through the day without delegating on a daily basis. MB*

Dyslexic entrepreneurs have harnessed their ability to **think differently**. They are prepared to trust their intuition when making business decisions. For instance, they pick good people as they know intuitively that a candidate will fit. Furthermore, they talk freely about seeing things differently when looking for solutions. This could be due to dyslexics having a propensity to be creative and display 'right brain' skills (Reid & Kirk, 2001).

> *Another thing that I think dyslexia has allowed me to do is see very quickly, if I'm talking with some software engineers, about the details of their code. I can see the whole picture of the software... I've been told that's very common for dyslexics. That is my skill. What I give to the team is that ability to see the whole picture. MB*

> *So I tend to think on my feet. I don't know what the decision is going to be until it's come out of my mouth. I make decisions fast and that is extremely useful in getting businesses off the ground. ZA*

> *I saw the opportunities that were, for me, wide open simply because other people all thought the same way. It's a very narrow road that they travel. JS*

*For me, being dyslexic means that it's a reason why I see things differently. And seeing things differently brings opportunities. AC*

## How can I be a successful entrepreneur?

Not all people who are dyslexic will be great at communication, delegation or have a fantastic creative ability, but think about your particular strengths and how you can use these to advantage. Also how might you overcome or compensate for weakness?

### Skills Checklist.

1. Find something you feel passionate about

2. Have a clear vision of what you wish to achieve

3. Communicate your vision to those around you

4. Carry out market research

5. Network to build useful contacts

6. Don't be afraid to ask for help

7. Identify what you do well and delegate the things you find difficult but keep overall control

8. Think about taking a partner into your business, someone who can compensate for your weaknesses

9. Work incredibly hard

10. Keep close to your customers and the market

11. Use your dyslexic advantage to make your business different to the competition.

Don't let a lack of confidence or fear of failure prevent you from launching your venture. We cannot be sure you will succeed, but put in safeguards to reduce the risk.

You might run your business in a part time capacity whilst you are still employed, to establish whether it will succeed.

Carry out as much market research as possible: It is very important to establish whether there is truly a market for your idea before you invest time and money.

Find something you feel really passionate about. If you enjoy your work you will not mind putting in long hours. All entrepreneurs work very hard at the beginning of their business. Being dyslexic means you will take longer to carry out some business related tasks but you will, conversely, do other things more quickly than others.

Remember you are probably able to see clearly how your business idea will work. Use your oral and persuasive skills to share your vision and encourage people to offer you support and advice. If you need to go to the bank for a loan or to an external investor your oral skills and ability to network will really help.

Consider either taking a partner into the business who can compensate for your weaknesses or think about employing someone to do the things you are not good at. Peter, an entrepreneur who recently sold his business for £5 million, struggled because of his dyslexia. He says:

> *The very first thing I did even when I ran the*
> *business from home was to employ a part-time*

*secretary/book keeper. This made my business look professional right from the start.*

Once your business is up and running, focus on the activities that you are really good at and make sure someone else is empowered to focus on the tasks you find hard. Do not neglect these tasks, check they are being done and maintain overall control if you wish to succeed.

You may lack confidence in your abilities at the start of your business, however, this is not a bad thing, this will keep you on your toes, scanning the environment and result in you being aware of changes and opportunities. Furthermore you are not alone, many successful dyslexic entrepreneurs say despite having made lots of money there are times when they still feel a lack of confidence.

**Overcoming dyslexic difficulties.**

Having had a rough time at school some dyslexics will not believe they can succeed. These feelings are hard to overcome, but careful planning, carrying out market research and getting advice from others will all help you to know whether your business idea can be successful and reduce the risk of failure.

Some dyslexics have a high need to achieve because school has left them feeling inadequate and scarred. Running your own business may be a way to channel your high need for achievement into something positive.

Other dyslexics feel angry about their dyslexia and some of the difficulties they have experienced as a result. Entrepreneurs succeed because they are driven and persevere. Channel your anger into positive energy for your business. Set your objectives and be determined to succeed.

## References.

Fitzgibbon, G. & O'Connor, B. (2002). *Adult Dyslexia: A Guide for the Workplace*. London: Wiley.

Hales, G. (1995). *Stress factors in the workplace*. In Miles, T.R. & Varma, V. (eds) (1995) *Dyslexia & Stress*. London: Whurr. pp. 74 – 82.

Logan, J. (2001). *Entrepreneurial success: A study of the incidence of dyslexia in the entrepreneurial population and the influence of dyslexia on success*. PhD thesis, Bristol University

Logan, J. (2009). *Dyslexic Entrepreneurs: the incidence, their coping strategies and their business skills. Dyslexia*, 15(4), pp.328–346

Logan, J. (2010). *What does Dyslexia Mean for Entrepreneurs and Successful Business Leaders?* International Dyslexia Conference 2010 Phoenix USA

Taylor, K. & Walter, J. (2003). *Occupation choices of adults with & without Dyslexia. Dyslexia: An International Journal of Research and Practice*, 9 (3).

### g. Personal experience: Setting up your own business.

**Lydia Mckee.**

### When were you diagnosed with dyslexia?

Aged about 8, when my mum sought a referral at school after concerns with my progress.

### How did your dyslexia affect you at work?

I had to fine tune my organisational skills because of my difficulties and this turned out to be an asset at work. It was an administration job so there was a lot of focus on my weaker areas such as spelling. However, forming good relationships with the people I worked with opened the way for asking for their support so that errors never left the office in correspondence with business partners. As I was working with creative people who often share similar difficulties, there were some who came to me for support with composing correspondence. It was a case of sharing strengths.

### Why did you decide to set up your own business?

I needed to find employment; I could have followed another administration role, but having experienced the build up stress that these roles cause me, the urge to follow my creative skills looked more inspiring. I had learnt from my jobs that I had the kind of self-discipline that is required to perpetuate the constant momentum that would be required.

### What was it like starting out on your own?

A bit scary at first but then I realised I have the freedom to make my own decisions about what happens and the directions I want to go in.

### What help did you receive?

The British Dyslexia Association mentoring scheme really helped me get my get my ideas down on paper and turn them in to actions but at the right points.

### Tell us a little bit about your business...

Sugar & Lace Cake Company (**www.sugarandlacecakecompany.co.uk**) is all about creating enjoyment for all occasions. That may be a cake for a wedding, a creative workshop, decorating cupcakes for a baby shower or hiring out an eclectic collection of crockery for an afternoon birthday party.

### Do you have any tips for other budding entrepreneurs?

Don't be afraid to talk to people about your ideas. I really found this helpful to me to get a feel for what people are looking for. Then research your ideas, look to see what others are doing – is there a gap – something they're not doing that you could?

# Chapter 4 – Further and Higher Education.

a. What should I know as a dyslexic adult starting higher/further education?

b. The Disabled Student Allowance (DSA)

c. How dyslexia might affect your studies and coping strategies

d. How can your institution help you?

e. Personal Experience: Further study

## a. What should I know as dyslexic adult starting higher/further education?
### Dr. Ross Cooper.

I approach the whole idea of coping strategies from the viewpoint that there is absolutely nothing wrong with being dyslexic. We are often very good indeed at lots of creative and problem solving activities. That's because those activities, like entrepreneurial business, comedy, design, story-telling, visual art, poetry, sport, song writing, engineering and acting can all suit the way we think. Never underestimate your talents.

The problem is that we are expected to do things and think like everyone else, and we find this difficult. So the starting point needs to be how can we get rid of the barriers that are disabling us?

### Your Learning.

Dyslexic learners are excellent learners if we are allowed to learn holistically. This means:

- following our passionate interests
- learning in bursts
- knowing why they are teaching what they are teaching
- allowing us to problem solve in our own ways
- learning by doing
- starting with what is meaningful before worrying about details
- You can't always say what you are thinking if you think visually (like most of us do), so give yourself

time to explain if necessary. Making a diagram can be better than words.

---

For more information:

## Study skills.

**Inclusive Solutions** – Learning style screening and information
**www.outsider.co-uk.com**

**Brain.HE** – information and resources for students including the holist manifesto, social model of disability
**www.brainhe.com**

**Super Reading** – Proof Reading courses
**www.outsider.co-uk.com/superreading**

Assistive technology:

**Emptech** – provides information on assistive technology
**www.emptech.info/index.php**

**B.D.A. new technology Committee** – provides information and reviews on assistive technology
**www.bdatech.org**

Equality act

**Equality Human Rights commission** – guidance on the Equality Act 2010 **http://www.equalityhumanrights. com/advice-and-guidance/new-equality-act-guidance/**

### Handling College or University.

Don't wait to until you 'fail' before asking for help. Be proactive and explain what you need and what is preventing you from learning, or being able to show what you have learned.

In Further Education (FE) & Higher Education (HE) 'learning support' is usually about building on your strengths and finding ways around barriers, rather than focusing on the things you find difficult.

If you are going to miss a deadline, always hand in what you have completed when asking for additional time.

Many dyslexic students find that screen readers are pretty hopeless as a substitute for reading except in emergencies, but great for proof reading our own writing.

Linear thinkers find it difficult to understand our difficulties with time and organisation, and can overreact and misinterpret our difficulties. It's best to avoid such misunderstandings. It can also be stressful, so use the counselling services to help you deal with any stress.

Disclosing your dyslexia at college or university is the best way of protecting your interests and getting the most out of your learning. There are hundreds of thousands of dyslexic students studying. You do not need to feel conspicuous, and spending more time with people who think like you can be a delight!

## b. The Disabled Students Allowance (DSA).

Dr. Ross Cooper.

**If you are going to Higher Education, claim your Disabled Students Allowance (DSA)!**

You may feel that you are not entitled to claim because you don't think of yourself as 'disabled'. The truth is we are being disabled all the time by people expecting us to be able to listen and take in long lectures, write our thoughts down under timed conditions and remember overlong verbal instructions. So while we may not think that dyslexia is a 'disability', we are certainly being disabled.

You would have thought that since this disabling process has occurred throughout our schooling, they might have given us a right to 'assistive technology' (isn't all technology assistive?) like laptops, screen readers and voice recognition from day one. But no, they reserve this for those of us who managed to get through to HE despite the disabling barriers. So make the most of it, you deserve it. And taking it does not take funds away from anyone else. 8 out of 10 people who get the DSA have a 'specific learning difficulty' – mostly dyslexia, and then dyspraxia, Asperger's, dyscalculia and Attention Deficit (Hyperactivity) Disorder/ AD(H)D.

**Getting the equipment and support takes around 6 months, so plan ahead and follow the DSA Chart, "Working with the DSA" (on page 70).**

When you meet with the Assessor of Need at the Access Centre, make sure that they have read the recommendations in your dyslexia assessment report. This will improve what they give you. Remember that they are not there to check whether or not you are dyslexic, but to give you what you need to overcome the barriers on your course. So it also helps to know what these are. They may be different for every course and learner.

---

For more information:

Go to:

**Disabled Student Allowance** – Government information on the Disabled Student Allowance **www.direct.gov.uk** (search disabled student allowance in the help box)

**Disabled Student Allowances Quality Assurances** – provides list of centres for DSA tests

**www.dsa-qag.org.uk**

---

# Working with the Disabled Students Allowance

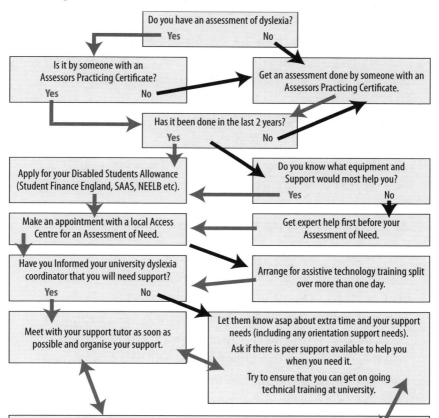

Do you have an assessment of dyslexia?
Yes    No

Is it by someone with an Assessors Practicing Certificate?
Yes    No

Get an assessment done by someone with an Assessors Practicing Certificate.

Has it been done in the last 2 years?
Yes    No

Apply for your Disabled Students Allowance (Student Finance England, SAAS, NEELB etc).

Do you know what equipment and Support would most help you?
Yes    No

Make an appointment with a local Access Centre for an Assessment of Need.

Get expert help first before your Assessment of Need.

Have you Informed your university dyslexia coordinator that you will need support?
Yes    No

Arrange for assistive technology training split over more than one day.

Meet with your support tutor as soon as possible and organise your support.

Let them know asap about extra time and your support needs (including any orientation support needs).

Ask if there is peer support available to help you when you need it.

Try to ensure that you can get on going technical training at university.

You have the right to use your DSA money to choose your own support tutor.

If the support provided is inadequate, you have the right to ask for more funds through the local Disability Officer (For example, most students are given a digital recorder for lectures which is not much use. Whereas with Audio Notetaker software, streams of recorded speech are transformed into editable coloured bars that you can navigate holistically and edit down quickly to the key points)

DSA can pay for any reasonable adjustment including specialised courses, 1:1 support, and more technology or software (up to a maximum amount of money)

Many students give up on speech recognition because they haven't been shown how to write formal text with it, or have not been shown how to keep the voice file 'clean' so that the recognition works efficiently. This simply takes more or better support.

universities can set whatever exams they like, these can be challenged if they disadvantage dyslexic students (ask if an Equality Impact Assessment has been done- this is a legal requirement to ensure that policies and decisions do not disable us)

Extra time is rarely enough for timed exams.
Look and ask for alternatives (like spoken exams, presentations, installations, etc.)

## c. How dyslexia might affect your studies.
### Sandra Hargreaves.

As a student with dyslexia, going to college or university is likely to be a challenging experience, but don't worry, it is for everyone else too. Don't feel daunted at the prospect; you just need to think about the strategies you will use to stop the experience from overwhelming you. Higher education is not like school where there is a lot of organisation in place and where there are teachers to help you. It is an environment in which you are largely left to your own devices and you must seek out the support, which is available. No one will come looking for you.

You need to register with Student Services for a screening test or assessment. If you have already been assessed, you need to present your assessment and to ask for an appointment for a Needs Assessment, so that you can be provided with the IT support and tutorial support you need through the **Disabled Students' Allowance (see previous section)**. This country is probably the best in the world at providing support for specific learning difficulties but you have to seek it out.

You will need to think about structuring your life, setting up timetables and schedules so you don't waste your time unnecessarily. You need to understand how you learn, so that you can apply your learning style to your work. You also need to understand which approach is best for you to gain the most out of the lectures and reading. You will be doing a lot of reading, so understanding how to get the most out of that is important to your success. You will also be doing a lot of writing. Even if you are artistic or practical, at university you have to be able to express yourself effectively, so your lecturers and examiners understand what you are trying to say. It doesn't matter how brilliant you are, if you can't convey that to others it will be lost to them.

**Organisation.**

The first thing you have to do is to put some very structured organisation into your life as it will possibly be the first time you have had to completely organise yourself. Where you had timetables at school which organised your week, you now only have the basic timetable of your lectures and tutorials. It is important to use your time very well so that you put down your study periods for each module and allow yourself some leisure, exercise and relaxation. This is also very important to your health and wellbeing.

The timetables below and on page 76 were compiled by a dyslexic student:

| | Monday | Tuesday | Wednesday | Thursday | Friday | Saturday | Sunday | | |
|---|---|---|---|---|---|---|---|---|---|
| 7 | | Running | | Running | | Running | | | |
| 8 | | | Yoga | | Yoga | | Yoga | | from............................ to............................ |
| 9 | ND213 Sports Nutrition | ND 208 Diet Therapy | | | PD 253 Admin in the NHS | Day Off | | | Weekly Targets: |
| 10 | | | | | | | | | |
| 11 | | | | | | | | | |
| 12 | | | | | | | | | |
| 1 | | | | | | | | | |
| 2 | Dyslexia | | | PD 252 Costing & Budgeting | FC 234 Food Processing | | | | |
| 3 | | | | | | | | | |
| 4 | | | | | | | | | |
| 5 | | | | | | | | | |
| 6 | | | | | | | | | |
| 7 | | | | | | | | | |
| evening | | | | | | | | | |

The first was done using Microsoft Excel and the second using Microsoft Word. The student has used colour/shading to block in the times not only for her lectures and tutorials, but to use the specific time indicated by the colour/shading to do assignments for that module and, later in the semester, to study for that subject if there are examinations. Timetables for examination preparation can also be made for the weeks leading up to the examination period and for the exams themselves. These timetables can be downloaded from the CDROM of *Study Skills for Students with Dyslexia* and amended for your own use.

| Time | Monday | Tuesday | Wednesday | Thursday | Friday | Saturday | Sunday |
|---|---|---|---|---|---|---|---|
| 9 | ND 214 Lecture | ND 211 Lecture | | ND 205 Lecture | | | |
| | | | 1.5 hrs Break | | | | |
| 10 | | | | | 2 hrs | | 2 hrs |
| | | | | | Break | | Break |
| 11 | | | | | | | |
| 12 | | | 2 hrs | | 1.5 hrs | | 1.5 hrs |
| | Lunch | Lunch | Lunch | Lunch | Lunch | | |
| 1pm | | | | Journey home | | | Lunch |
| | Dyslexia | | | | | | |
| 2 | Journey home | Library FC220 Lecture | | | | | 1.5 hrs |
| 3 | | | 1.5 hrs Break | 2 hrs Break | 1.5 hrs Break | Day Off Work | Break |
| 4 | 2 hrs | | | | | | |
| | | Journey home | | | | | |
| 5 | Dinner | | 2 hrs | 1.5 hrs | 2 hrs | | 2 hrs |
| 6 | | Dinner | Dinner | Dinner | Dinner | | Dinner |
| | 1.5 hrs | | | Dance | | | |
| 7 | | | | | | | |
| 8 | | 2 hrs Break | 2 hrs Break | Pilates | | | 2 hrs Break |
| 9 | Yoga | | | | | | |
| | | 1 hr | 1 hr | | | | 1 hr |
| 10 | | | | Break | Night Off | | |

## Learning Style.

Another important step is to ascertain your learning style if you don't already know it, that is to think about and work out whether you learn best by visual, auditory or kinaesthetic methods. There are many questionnaires to help you come to an understanding of how you learn and the following charts show you some of the ways you can learn in your preferred style.

## Visual

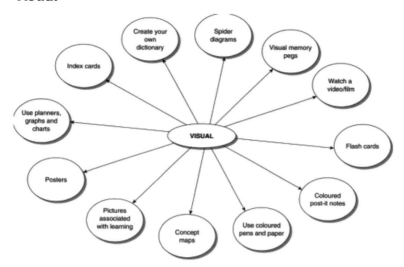

## Auditory

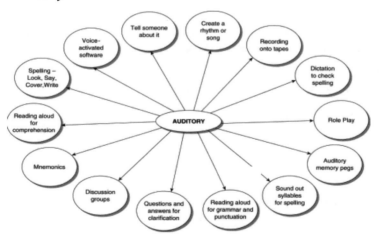

## Kinaesthetic

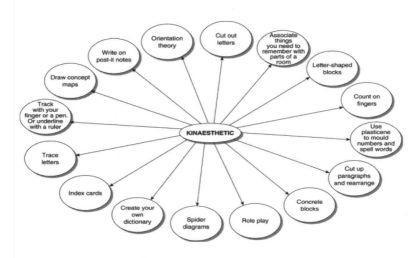

## Note Taking and Note Making.

It is also important to work out the best way for you to make notes in lectures and tutorials according to your learning style and also whether you like to use technology. If you are a visual learner you may prefer to use concept maps and if you are an auditory learner you may like to record your notes to replay later. This is a complex topic and you can learn more about it by referring to Chapter 3 of *Study Skills for Students with Dyslexia*.

## Reading.

Reading is essential at university and there are many ways you can help yourself improve your reading. It is important to have a strategy so that you are reading effectively and not just sitting staring at the text. There are many strategies but one of the best is the **SQ3R** Method, which suggests that you look over (or skim) the text you are reading (**Survey**), that you pose a **Question** for your reading and that you **Read** carefully for meaning, you then **Recall** your thoughts to answer the question you have posed and you **Review** the text, critically thinking about whether you agree with the point of view given. There are also useful software packages to help you with reading such as *Texthelp Read and Write* and *Claroread*.

**Essay Writing.**

This is an essential skill to master, as most of your assessments will depend on your ability to write fluent and coherent essays, putting your points across systematically and logically. There are many ways of tackling essay writing but they all involve a close analysis of the question, working out exactly what it is asking you to do. It is then essential to work out the type of answer you will need to prepare and to put down all the issues or themes involved with the answer. Many students find it useful to prepare a mind map at this stage either by hand or electronically using one of the excellent software packages available such as *Inspiration* or *MindManager*. More information can be found in Chapter 5 of *Study Skills for Students with Dyslexia*.

**Conclusion.**

Don't let the thought of going to university make you stressed. You can succeed by having the right mind-set and learning strategies, which will help you. With the help of a dyslexia tutor and assistive technology, which you are entitled to under the **Disabled Students' Allowance (DSA)** you will

find that you will enjoy your time at university.  In
fact it may be the best time in your whole life.

## References:

Hargreaves, S (2012) *Study Skills for students
with dyslexia* London: Sage

Further Information:

**Disabled Student Allowance** – Government information on the Disabled Student Allowance – **www.direct.gov.uk** (search disabled student allowance in the help box)

**Disabled Student Allowances Quality Assurances** – provides list of centres for DSA tests **www.dsa-qag.org.uk**

**Into Higher Education guide** – Higher education guide for people with disabilities – **www.disabilityrightsuk. org/intohighereducation2012.htm**

**Disabled student allowance** **www.direct.gov. uk/en/DisabledPeople/EducationAndTraining/ HigherEducation/DG_10034898**?

Assistive technology:

**B.D.A. new technology Committee** – provides information and reviews on assistive technology – **www.bdatech.org**

**Texthelp read and Write Gold** – text to speech software – **www.texthelp.com/UK**

**ClaroRead** – text to speech software – **www.clarosoftware.com**

**Inspiration** – Mind Mapping software – **www.inspiration.com**

**MindManager** – Mind Mapping software – **www.mindjet.com**

## d. How can your institution help you?
**Heather Evans.**

Photos by Mark Wright & Billy Moore.

Entering a college of further education can, particularly for a learner with dyslexia, be a daunting prospect. This article aims to reassure you that further education colleges are well equipped to address your needs and to support you throughout your time in college.

First of all as a student in F.E. you will be given the opportunity to disclose your learning needs and then to discuss any difficulties you have with a specialist.

### Initial assessment of need.

You may know before you arrive that you are dyslexic. If so we will talk with you about the previous assessment and any support that you have had, what worked and what didn't work. We will discuss a suitable package of support with you.

If you have not had a diagnosis but have experienced persistent difficulties with your studies we will assess you and make some recommendations.

### Exam Access Arrangements.

If you are taking any examinations whilst you are at the college an assessment will be carried out to determine what type of exam access arrangements are relevant to your needs. Where a scribe or reader is recommended we make arrangements for learners to practise using these before taking their examination.

**Additional support arrangements.**

There are several types of support that can be put in place. Each student will be assessed and an appropriate package of support will be offered. Below are some of the ways you may be supported:

1. **One-to-one support with a specialist tutor** – this type of support is useful if you have difficulties with:
   - writing assignments, essays,
   - writing things in your own words, say from a textbook or an internet page,
   - spelling,
   - reading and understanding assignment briefs,
   - organising yourself for study e.g. time management, prioritising workload, revision techniques.

2. **Small group support in a workshop** – depending on level of individual needs. You may find this type of support helpful if you have difficulties with:
   - expressing your views and ideas in front of other students,
   - presenting your work to others,
   - revision techniques.

3. **Support in class** – this type of support can be useful if you have difficulties with:
   - taking notes in class – e.g. a note-taker can do this for you

- understanding a task – a learning facilitator can check your understanding by explaining it in a different way or by asking you to explain what you think you need to do,

- remembering instructions given to you in class – a learning facilitator can write down tasks for you and help you to put them in priority order, reading and understanding an assignment brief – a learning facilitator can prompt you to highlight the important points and/or explain it in a simpler, more straightforward way.

**Strategies might include:**

- Higher order study strategies such as the higher order reading skills of skimming, scanning and close reading to improve your confidence with reading for study purposes,

- Spelling strategies – a range of strategies to help you to improve your spellings,

- Ways to improve your written expression,

- Higher order thinking skills – to help you to improve your ability to problem solve and manage more complicated study tasks as well as improving your memory,

- Organisation, target setting and time management – these are skills that a lot of people have difficulty with but they are important and can help make studying a lot less stressful

- Planning and concept mapping techniques – these skills are very useful for people who find it difficult to know how to start a piece of writing and/or have difficulties getting their ideas on to paper.

**Equipment might include:**

- Loans of equipment such as digital voice recorders – these can be helpful if you can't catch everything that is said in class or have difficulties taking notes

- Use of specialist software e.g. text-to-speech or speech to text– this software can help you to:

  o read research articles or longer pieces of text,

  o proofread your own assignments or essays,

  o write essays, assignments, reports.

- Overlays for learners who experience visual disturbance when they read.

- Tracking rulers for learners who find it difficult to keep track of where they are in text.

- Memory sticks with a range of free downloads such as concept mapping software, text-to-speech software.

**Full diagnostic assessments.**

If you are planning to go on to higher education after your course we will make sure that we complete a full diagnostic assessment so that you are eligible to apply for Disabled Student's Allowance (DSA). DSA is a fund which can provide you with the necessary support and equipment, such as computer software, to help you with your studies in higher education.

**Moving on to Higher Education.**

To help you to prepare for moving on to higher education you will be encouraged to continue attending support at college. Our aim throughout your studies is to help you to overcome any anxieties you may have about study and to become an independent learner so that you can feel in control of your studies and equipped with the skills you will need for studying at a higher level.

## e. Personal experience: further study.

Chris Rossiter.

### When were you diagnosed with dyslexia?

November 2010, age 29

### What further/higher education are you doing?

I am a current occupational psychology and management science PhD student at the University of Surrey. The focus of my research is on employees with a non-visible disability and their experiences of organisational decision making.

### How has dyslexia affected your further/higher education?

This is a difficult question to answer. Really, my dyslexia does not have a great impact on my day-to-day activities. Of course, I make spelling mistakes and my reading speed could be improved, but overall it's not a problem. However dyslexia has affected my confidence and my determination. You might say that this is not a direct effect of dyslexia, rather my own reaction to how I feel about it. I'm really determined to prove that I'm as able and intelligent as anyone else, although it has taken me a long time to realise that this is about proving this to myself and not a competition.

### What support have you received?

I received DSA last year and have received some IT equipment and one-to-one support. This has been a real help and made my work much easier.

## What support/assistive technology have you found most useful?

My digital voice recorder is the best thing I have. I did receive copies of Dragon, Read & Write Gold (RWG) and MindView, but I use these less often. Generally I'll create a concept-map early on in a project and then use Dragon and RWG as I'm working. Although none of these is as good as my recorder. I carry this with me, especially if I go to a meeting, and record my thoughts straight away. Dictating is beneficial as I can record my thoughts quicker than writing them down. It also helps clear my mind as I can often get carried away with ideas, which is both distracting and tiring.

## What strengths do you think your dyslexia given you?

I do not think my dyslexia affords me any special abilities, to me that's not how it works. My dyslexia is just one part of me. I do not equate my strengths with dyslexia, because this suggests it has a greater effect on me than I think it actually does. However, it has affected my confidence and made me more determined as a way of proving myself.

## Do you have any advice for dyslexic adults who want to continue their education?

Do it! I had completed my first degree, at the age of 29, before discovering my dyslexia. My school days and performance at GCSE and A-Level were strictly mediocre and this left me feeling disappointed. I always considered myself to be intelligent but I was never any good at putting this into practice. I was constantly frustrated by my own inability to write in a succinct and coherent way. As I've got older this has become much easier. I know that people often say that learning is easier when you're young. However as you get older it's much easier to discern and question the information you're presented with. Being critical is not only an essential academic skill it is also a key way of learning and dissecting information.

**Lydia Townsend.**

### When were you diagnosed with dyslexia?

When I was eight years old I was diagnosed as being dyslexic. I was a keen writer at that time, plagiarised books about bunny rabbits mostly, and as such it was decided my love of words meant I was mildly dyslexic at worst. My reading was inconsistent, my written words illigible, my spellings creative at best, my grammar atrocious, still I wrote stories constantly. It was 'common knowledge' (incorrectly) then that children couldn't love writing if they were dyslexic.

### How did you find education? What support did you receive?

It is hard to look back at my compulsory schooling. I can honestly say I hated it. Even in infant school my 'laziness' in literacy had left me sat writing alone while the other children were allowed to move on to other tasks. Now I am about to start my third year reading a combined honours Education and Psychology degree. I consistently get high grades and I enjoy every minute of it. My situation couldn't be more different. I was lucky. At the age of 16, with my elder sister Amy (another academically high achieving school failing dyslexic) in toe, I managed to talk my way onto the International Baccalaureate (IB) course despite not having good enough grades. Though I didn't have specific dyslexia support, the teachers I had took my academic talents and helped me fall back in love with learning. I even managed to learn a second language!

I didn't receive support during my mainstream schooling, nor during college. I got given extra time in a few exams but I am not sure that really counts. To be quite frank even if I had been offered support I doubt I would have taken it. The attitude of many of my teachers was that dyslexia is simply an excuse to be lazy. I was mortified one French lesson when I was taken outside by my teacher and told to stop using my dyslexia as an excuse for laziness.

I was prevented from being in the top class for English in secondary school because, as my headmaster stated, 'clever kids don't have learning difficulties.' I didn't want to be a dyslexic and I certainly didn't want anyone to know I had what I saw as an awful condition.

**My advice on further and higher education?**

Don't take no for an answer. If you are told being dyslexic means you can't do something go ahead and do it anyway. Be proud of being dyslexic. See it as advantage rather than a hindrance. Thinking differently gets you far further in life than following the crowd. Also make sure there is adequate dyslexia support in the institution you intend to go to; the support I have now received at university has been invaluable.

At the age of eighteen, after starting university, I was re-assessed and my dyslexia diagnosis was changed to severe. As it turns out, being good at putting words into a story does not stop you being dyslexic.

# Chapter 5 – Coping strategies for daily life.

**Eorann Lean.**

a.  Family and Friends

b.  At home administration

c.  Dealing with other organisations

d.  Transport and directions

Dyslexia isn't only a factor during education or at work – it's there every day. From navigating the transport system to paying bills daily life can be affected by dyslexia. However as long as tasks are approached appropriately there are ways, as in education and work, of dealing with the difficulties.

## a. Family and friends.

### Arriving on time.

- Focus on a different time than the start time

This can be done by either having a 'departure time' or a 'fake start time' in your head. When you are first arranging the meeting or told of the event, spend some time working out how long it will take you to get there from your house (or wherever you will be beforehand), then build in 10 minutes for any problems (traffic, trying to find the keys etc). This is the 'departure time' you need to write down in your diary.

If you don't have time to do this then take away 10 or 15 minutes from the actual start time and write this down in your diary. This will have built you in extra time.

- Set alarms

Set two alarms. One 10 minutes before you need to leave so that you have time to get your things together and one when you need to leave the house.

### Remembering Birthdays.

- Calendars and reminders

This can be a paper calendar on a wall or book but an electronic one is the easier option as they don't rely on you checking them. Electronic calendars can be set up to send you reminder emails or notifications on your phone. Many internet calendars are also able to synchronise with phone calendar to help you be organised. Reminders can then be set to a week before so you have time to buy a present or on the day to remind you to be in contact.

- Electronic cards

There are also now many email greeting card services that will send the card on a date you put in so you can set it up in advance rather than relying on remembering on the day.

### Borrowing and Lending.

Borrowing a good CD, film or just £5 because you've left your wallet at home is a normal part of friendship but it can become difficult very quickly when you can't remember what you've borrowed or from whom. Worse still when you've lent something to someone you won't even have the help of them asking for it back.

- Record book

Make a note of it straight away either on a recording device or notebook. If the lender would like it back at a certain point write this in your calender and set a reminder. You may also find it useful to make a reminder for a month after the object has been lent to ask for it back. Even if you don't want it back then it will keep it fresh in your mind so when you do need it you know where it is.

## b. At home.

### Post.

It's very easy to let post build up into a mountain that needs opening and sorting. Of course

once it gets to that stage it's even easier to
put it off because it's such a big task.

- Split the task

The best thing to do to deal with post is to split the tasks
into opening it, sorting it and dealing with it. Be strict
with yourself and always open post when it comes in. A
quick glance should help you see if it needs replying to,
reading, filing for further reference or throwing away.

- Expanding file

Sorting it can then be done by having an expanding file
for important letters and information to be kept in and
an in-tray for 'to be dealt with' letters. Bank statements,
tickets or anything you need to find again but don't
need to be addressed immediately go in the file. If the
letter needs further action then this can be put in the
in-tray. This should already reduce your post mountain

- In-tray

To deal with the in-tray assign a specific administration
(admin.) time once a week as detailed below.

**Bills.**

- Direct debit

Probably the easiest way to manage bills is to set
up direct debits to pay them so that you don't have
to struggle with them. It is also possible to get a
discount on certain bills if you set up a direct debit.

- Regularity

For those bills that cannot be done by direct debit
then it is important to organise a regular time
when you pay off bills and keep on top of them, for
instance allocate yourself an admin. hour weekly.

**Admin. time and to-do lists.**

- Admin. hour

There are many necessary everyday tasks that need
focus in your free time such as sorting post, paying bills,
returning a phone call and booking appointments. It can
be very hard to fit these in and to manage to sit down to
them. A regular time for administration makes dealing
with these items part of your routine and gives you a
time when you can concentrate on just the tasks at hand.
How long your time is depends on how much you get in
but an hour a week should help you keep on top of it.

- To do list

Of course tasks will not always come in when you're at
home next to your in-tray, we've all sat on a train and
suddenly realised there is something we need to do.
A portable to do list (whether a notebook, recording
device or electronic on a phone or computer) means
you can jot something down as soon as you think of
it, rather than trying to remember it or having to deal
with it straight away (and therefore distracting yourself
from other tasks). You can then deal with the items on
your to do list during your admin. time – the list will
also help you work more efficiently during the hour.

## c. Other organisations.

### Appointments.

As well as making a calendar event and reminder for appointments many places such as dentists and doctors will give you a call or text to remind you a day or so before of your appointment.

### Restaurants.

If you are struggling reading a menu you can ask the waiter if they have any suggestions which should give you some of the highlights from the menu.

## d. Transport.

### Learning to Drive.

Your dyslexia may mean that you take longer to learn to drive and need more than one attempt to pass your test. This is because dyslexic learners are likely to need lots of reinforcement to embed learning from the short term memory to their often excellent long term memory.

- Talk to your instructor

Tell your instructor that you are dyslexic and how you learn best. This may mean asking them to only give one instruction at a time if possible or tying information to a memory anchor such as a rhyme or rhythm.

- Direction help

If you have difficulty with your left and right make this easier by writing L on your left hand and R on your right or put colour stickers on the dashboard. You can also ask your instructor and tester to give you directions in a way you will understand as in 'the next left which is by the cinema.' If you find it useful you can ask your examiner to show you a simple diagram before the independent driving section so you can visualise your route.

- Theory Test

Dyslexic candidates can apply to have up to double the standard 40 minutes. You need to ask when you apply for the test. A letter or report from a professional should explain your reading ability, i.e. a teacher, a psychologist, or Local Dyslexia Association officer. The Driving Standards Agency has also agreed to accept the report from The British Dyslexia Association's online screening test Spot Your Potential which you can find on our website. You will have to phone again for a test date after the report has been processed.

Dyslexic candidates also have the option of listening to the test being read in English through a headset.

**Train Journeys.**

- Personal timetables

The National rail website offers the ability to create your own personal 'pocket timetable.' This means that you can read (or listen with text read back if you have it) and familiarise yourself with your journey before you start on it. Furthermore it gives you something to check if you forget what time your train is. The timetable can also be shown to station staff so they can help you get to the correct station. The 'pocket timetable' does not only give you times but you can also see the train stations that the train passes through so you will know when your nearing your destination.

- Phone apps

There are also many train apps for phones that can help you, including providing timetables like the printable ones above, when your next train is (based on your location), an alarm that goes off before your station and more.

## Bus Journeys.

- Ask the driver

These can be more difficult and what there is to help you depends on each local service. However there is the added bonus of being able to interact with the driver. The simplest thing to do if you are not sure of your journey is to tell the driver where you are trying to get to and ask if they could tell you when you're there. Most drivers are used to this and will help you.

- Ring ahead

If you are worried about getting from one service to another you can ring ahead and have someone meet you from the bus.

## Directions.

- Smart phones

Most smart phones now have GPS applications so that you can find yourself on a map and get directions. The very helpful part of this feature is that you can track where you are going on the map and so see if you have turned in the wrong direction.

- Maps from the computer

However, there are other options, such as using Google maps on a computer beforehand which will give walking, cycling and driving directions. You can then print off these instructions along with a map which you can use to familiarise yourself with your route before you leave and take it with you to help you navigate.

- Asking people

If you find yourself lost in a city either find a cab driver (they have a great knowledge of their area and will be able to point you in the right direction) or a hotel who will be used to giving their customers directions and may have maps.

For more information:

## Go to:

**Google Calendar** – Electronic calendars
**www.google.com/calendar**

**Driving tests**

**DSA app Theory Test for Car Drivers Kit**: – for theory test revision available from iTunes store

**Driving Test Success by Focus Software** – highly recommended by driving instructors experienced in candidates with specific learning difficulties. Available from Amazon.

**DSA** – to ask for extra time or a voiceover during your theory test 0300-200-1122 **www.direct.gov.uk**

## Train timetables and apps

**www.Nationalrail.co.uk** (travel tools at the bottom of home page)

## Phone Apps

**2 Do app** – good interface for creating lists – **www.2doapp.com/**

**Quinnscape** – useful for helping you pack and remember to bring things: **www.quinnscape.com/**

**Epic Win** – A game style to do list app – **itunes. apple.com/gb/app/epicwin/id372927221?mt=8**

**Evernote** – helps you remember thoughts, ideas and people with text, photos and audio – **www.evernote.com**

**Expense manager** – Money organising app for android – **play.google.com/store/apps/details?id=com. expensemanager&hl=en**

**Mint money manager** – Money organising for smart phones and computer – **www.mint.com/t/012/**

# Chapter 6 – Assistive Technology.

**By Arran Smith.**
**Edited by E.A. Draffan and Laura Merceron.**

a. Spelling Support

b. Text to speech software

c. Speech to text software

d. Voice recorders and note taking support

e. Ipads and smart phones

f. How can I be involved in social media?

## Assistive Technology.

Assistive technology is not necessarily a specialist software item or even a specific specialist device, it is just something that might make life easier or help you with a particular task. The type of technologies that come under this umbrella term have become more mainstream over the years and now we take it for granted that computers can read out text or mobile phones will offer us reminders.

However, one of the most important things to reflect upon when considering the use of assistive technology is the training needed to support your choices and needs. Some technologies can be complex but offer a wide range of options that can provide you with useful strategies – just trying some technologies for the first time does not always show them in the best light.

There are a number of assistive hardware and software solutions to support all aspects of dyslexia, including assistance with spelling, sequencing, memory and grammar. They include solutions such as text to speech and speech to text software as well as reminders, diary aids and project management tools.

My aim is to take you through some hardware and software that work well for me in a project led, office and computer based environment. I must state that not all support is technological. I have found that the best solution to correct syntax in documents is to have an 'Access to Work' support worker; my support worker assisted with the editing this chapter.

## a. Spelling support.

### WordShark.

Before I started work and was worried about my spelling accuracy, I used to use Wordshark. It was developed by Whitespace and is an interactive software application that uses multi-sensory games. It can be used by individuals of any age range, but has been specifically designed for younger children based on a basic program for improving reading, spelling, memory and phonics (individual sounds). It is based on 9000 useful words, but you can program words appropriate to your circumstances into it. The software has been developed using a structured program called Alpha to Omega, that is valid for use up to the GCSE curriculum (Key Stage 3). It is a useful aid within specialist teaching programs. At the end of each learning game, the individual is rewarded with a computerised game.

Results can be generated to create a personal history for each subject showing individual improvement, and is best used when incorporated within a structured program as an added benefit.

### Touch Type Read and Spell (TTRS).

This piece of software does exactly what it says on the tin. It supports learners at a basic level with typing, in a multi-sensory way, with auditory commentary and visual clues. The program begins with a basic window which builds up over time, enabling touch typing and spelling.

It builds vocabulary by **seeing words** correctly spelled, singularly and in sentences, **hearing words** spoken by the program, and **touching words** (kinaesthetics), using typing, to aid memory for spelling words.

It follows the phonetic progression found in 'Alpha to Omega'.

This product can be used in multiple environments, and in my opinion, is a very valuable, basic beginner program for dyslexics to learn to use a computer keyboard.

### Global AutoCorrect.

This product has been designed by a dyslexic to help you write without 'losing the flow' when the squiggly line of the spell checker stops your thoughts. Like Microsoft Autocorrect it runs as a background program and automatically corrects simple, often used words. But Global Autocorrect incorporates a further function, which records words that are frequently incorrectly spelled by the individual, using the program. It creates a list for individuals to 'learn from their mistakes'. This functionality has the ability to lessen frustration, and make creating a written piece of work less daunting for the dyslexic.

## b. Text to speech software.

These products assist dyslexics with reading on the computer. The products below produce text to speech, which is an audio output from typed text. This includes products such as 'ClaroRead' and 'Texthelp' Read and Write, Dolphin Computer Access 'SaySo' and Don Johnston's 'Read:OutLoud'. These all have many other options including text highlighting, dictionaries and further proofreading support, as well as a choice of real-time voices. The two products I have used are:

### ClaroRead.

This runs as a background program on your computer, and enables you to highlight a section of computer based text. It will then read the text back to you. Claro converts PDFs into accessible formats providing a choice of voices as well as speed and pausing controls.

ClaroRead can be most useful when using the Internet. You can highlight a section of text and Claro automatically reads it back. When used in conjunction with a word processor, settings can be set to read each word that you type as you write, or to read back each sentence to you. This very much depends on your style of working, but the choice is there. In this way, Claro enables independent working, however it does not correct syntax mistakes.

### Texthelp Read and Write Gold.

Texthelp Read and Write Gold also runs as a background program on your computer, and includes a Text-to-Speech function with synchronized highlighting. It works on a similar basis to ClaroRead, with added functionality of a Screenshot Reader, Screen Masking and a PDF reading section. It also has an auto-correction spelling tool which contains a vocabulary list builder, as well as a picture dictionary and a pronunciation tutor.

When using Texthelp Read and Write Gold online, or in Microsoft Word, it synchronises highlighting the text with the spoken word and this helps to deal with visual tracking difficulties.

**Scan to Read.**

Intel Reader has been designed to capture digital images of the written page and 'read them back to you' whilst displaying the text for you to follow. This is useful as it can capture an image of two pages of full text.

OCR is also incorporated into the LG Scanner Mouse, which is a mouse with an inbuilt scanner. The software means that you can scan a part of a book, highlight the required section, and this will be converted into text. You can then use products such as Texthelp Read and Write or ClaroRead for text to speech.

## c. Speech to text software.

### Dragon NaturallySpeaking from Nuance.

This program converts speech to text. You dictate sentences, if possible with added punctuation or pauses, into your computer through a high quality microphone. The software then converts this to text. The product can also be used for voice commands to enable your computer to carry out specific functions.

As a severe dyslexic, I use Dragon NaturallySpeaking, however, I do find it quite frustrating on the odd occasion. Dragon is not like a human, we can separate sounds and words. If you are speaking to your friend, and your mother is shouting at you, you can easily separate who is speaking. When using Dragon, you have to speak very specifically, only letting it hear exactly what you want it to type. The product does take time to train and I would recommend that you have outside training and support on the software to use it to its full advantage.

Dragon has also released an app for your iPhone, iPad and iPod Touch allowing you to dictate short sentences which it turns into text, which you can use to send emails and also update Facebook and Twitter, but you must be connected to the internet for this to work.

## d. Voice recorders and note-taking help.

A number of recording devices can be used to support dyslexia, such as Olympus Voice Recorders which digitally record meetings or reminders. These can be used in conjunction with Dragon NaturallySpeaking, but once again it is advisable to train the software using the voice recorder microphone to provide the best results.

### Audio Notetaker.

This enables the user to directly record conversations and lectures through a high quality microphone plugged into a lap-top and to download the audio files at a later time. The software breaks down the voice recording, enabling you to add notes, colour code sections and import PowerPoint presentations to support or recall the events.

### Live Scribe.

The pen uses special paper that you write on and the pen records what you've written. It also records the audio at the same time. If you then tap the page where you have written something but can't remember the audio, it plays back the audio from that point in your notes. This is useful for students going to lectures who can't make notes at speed or as an aide memoire for meeting minutes. A voice recorder which records the whole conversation is unable to link audio to written work in the same way.

## e. iPads and smart phones.

The iPad is incredibly portable and turns on almost instantaneously, making it much more convenient than a laptop. The fast turn on means there is no frustrating wait to access what you need or difficulty remembering the idea you want to write down, as in two taps you're noting it down. Furthermore it is a single application device – one program is opened on the screen at a time, compared to a laptop where many things can be open on the screen at once. This is important as it cuts down on visual stress and distraction.

There are a number of useful apps that can be downloaded from the Apple store to your iPad, such as Claro Speak, that will read aloud any text on the iPad. However many useful accessible features are already built in, such as Voiceover (which reads your emails to you by the paragraph, but does not offer synchronised highlighting), black or white background and zoom in and out. This has not been designed specifically for dyslexics but can be useful and supportive in certain situations.

Smart phones are a really useful tool for dyslexics with many apps helping with organisation, to do lists, spelling, dictating etc. I find the iPhone 4s particularly useful as it runs Siri, which is very supportive as you can use it as a personal assistant by asking diary and information questions, such as 'what will the weather be like at 2pm'? 'What time is my meeting with Adam?'

When using a mobile device such as an iPhone, I would recommend a cloud based e-mail service to support with planning and organisation: products such as Gmail, icloud, Microsoft exchange and VM Ware's Zimbra email. These products offer email, calendar and reminder tools which sync with all devices. If you enter a meeting diary on your iPhone, this will appear on your computer and online, enabling you to plan and organise effectively.

## f. How can I be involved in social media?

Social media is becoming a large part of everyday life for the modern individual, and as a dyslexic it is difficult to be included with so much text flying around. Audioboo is a website which has free registration and enables you to create an audio blog or a podcast that can be submitted to Twitter and Facebook. As a dyslexic I find this invaluable, and when I am at an event, there is no need for me to write a blog about it when I can just say one.

In conclusion, there are many types of assistive software and hardware for dyslexic people. Not every dyslexic will find the technologies easy, but it is worth perseverance. Training is the most important undertaking along with making the right choices. These are some of the assistive technologies that I have found useful for my dyslexia but get advice from experts, speak to friends and try before you buy! These are all my personal recommendations, but other good products are available.

Lots more information can be found at **www.bdatech.org**

For further information

## Go to:

Word Shark – **programme to help with learning spelling**

**www.wordshark.co.uk**
ClaroRead – text to speech software

**www.clarosoftware.com**
Texthelp read and Write Gold – Text to speech software

**www.texthelp.com/UK**

**Dragon NaturallySpeaking** – Speech to text software

**www.nuance.com/dragon**

**Live Scribe** – Note taking software

**www.livescribe.com/uk/**

**B.D.A. new technology Committee** – provides information and reviews on assistive technology

**www.bdatech.org**

# Chapter 7 – Success.

a. The principles of success

b. Left behind at the beginning of the race: the paradoxes of dyslexia

c. Personal Experience

## a. The principles of success – what psychology tells us about achievement, happiness and fulfilment.
**Professor Patrick W. Jordan.**

Positive psychology is a new branch of psychology which deals with why some people are happier, more successful and more fulfilled than others. It can be thought of as an academic version of self-help.

Researchers have done many hundreds of studies in this area, looking at lots of different issues including how to have a successful career, a happy family life, good friendships and fulfilling hobbies and leisure time.

They found that there are five key principles which, if we apply them consistently, can increase the chances of our achieving success and happiness in all areas of our lives.

They are:

**PRINCIPLE 1. TAKE RESPONSIBILITY.**

Understand that we, and nobody else, are responsible for our actions, thoughts and attitudes. We should actively try to make our lives the best they can be.

**Top tip.**

When things aren't going as well as we would like in our lives, instead of asking ourselves 'why' questions we should ask 'how' questions.

Why questions can lead to self-pity, but 'how' questions lead to action

For example:

Replacing 'why' questions with 'how' questions.

| Replace... | With... |
|---|---|
| Why is my career going so badly? | How can I make my career go better? |
| Why do my relationships never work out? | How can I make my next relationship work? |
| Why do I never have the time to do the things I want to? | How can I find the time to do the things I want to? |
| Why do I have so many disadvantages in life? | How can I overcome the disadvantages I have? |

## PRINCIPLE 2. SET GOALS.

Goals provide us with a direction in life. They help us to focus our energy on what is important to us. We need to make decisions about what we want from life and to set clear goals that reflect this.

### Top tip.

Write the obituary that you would like to have after you have died.

Consider

- What would you like it to contain?
- Whatever you put in this are probably the things that are really important to you.
- Make sure you prioritise them when setting your life goals.

## PRINCIPLE 3. BE POSITIVE.

Having a positive, optimistic outlook makes life more enjoyable for us and for those around us. It also gives us energy and drive, making us far more likely to be successful.

**Top Tip.**

Be grateful and savour the good things and experiences that you have in your life.

- When something good happens make sure you appreciate the moment.
- Tell your friends about the good things that happen to you.
- When it is something extra-special have a celebration such as drinks out with friends or a party.
- At the end of each day think of three things that have happened that you can be grateful for.

### PRINCIPLE 4. PERSEVERE INTELLIGENTLY.

Getting the most from life requires determination and perseverance. It also requires a flexible and intelligent approach to life. If a course of action doesn't work, we must be able to find effective alternatives.

**Top Tip.**

Find out what you love most and are best at and develop your strengths.

If you are good at something and love doing it keep doing it, get even better at it and think how you could use this strength to achieve your goals.

For example

| If you are good at... | Think how you use this to... |
|---|---|
| Giving presentations | Can help you in your career |
| Practical things | Help people and demonstrate friendship |
| Being creative | Enjoy new hobbies and activities |
| Listening to and understanding people | Help people with their problems |

## PRINCIPLE 5. CONNECT WITH PEOPLE.

None of us lives in isolation. To be successful we need to have effective relationships with other people in all areas of our professional and personal lives.

### Top Tip.

Treat others as you would like them to treat you.

- Be the friend that you would like your friends to be to you.

- Show your partner the consideration you would like them to show to you.

- Behave at work as you would like your colleagues to behave towards you.

- Treat the weakest in society with the compassion you would like to be shown if you fell on hard times.

- And understand that the secret of being charismatic – make other people feel good about themselves.

We can never guarantee a totally happy or successful life. However hard we try there may be some things that we can't manage to achieve and other things that are simply beyond our control.

Nevertheless, if we remember the principles of success and apply them consistently in our lives, we will maximise the changes of having a happy, successful and fulfilling life and of being the best we can be.

1. Take responsibility

2. Set goals

3. Be positive

4. Persevere intelligently

5. Connect with others

**For more information**

**Read:**

**The Principles of Success by Professor Patrick Jordan. Published by WWPC Ltd.**

## b. Left behind at the beginning of the race: the paradoxes of dyslexia.
**Thomas G. West.**

The beginning is familiar. The story of a little boy who could hardly read at all for the first three or four years of primary school – and struggled for many years to keep up. For a long time, his greatest ambition was to not be at the bottom of the class.

Gradually, however, as the curriculum changed from rote memorization to larger concepts and logical thinking, the little boy began to see that he could do easily things that his classmates had trouble with – and that he could quickly see things that they did not easily see.

Over time, amazingly, this little boy became an author of books about dyslexia, visual talents and emerging computer graphic technologies. His writing led to invitations to give many talks, including talks in 17 foreign countries. His first book has been translated into three languages – Japanese, Chinese and, most recently, Korean. To his surprise (and to the delight of his publisher), over time his first book became a classic – an "evergreen," as they say in the trade, a book that never stops selling.

"I was happy as a child… I have been happier every year since I became a man. But this interlude of school [made] a sombre grey patch upon the chart of my journey… All my contemporaries and even younger boys seemed in every way better adapted to the conditions of our little world. They were far better both at the games and the lessons. It is not pleasant to feel oneself so completely outclassed and left behind at the beginning of the race."

These are not my words. However, these words perfectly reflect my own feelings through most of my own early education. They are the words of Winston Churchill writing in 1930 of his own early life. At this point, Churchill was a well known public figure – indeed, one who many thought was well past his prime – although his greatest test and his chief accomplishments were not to unfold until nine years later with the beginning of World War II. (Churchill, *My Early Life*, 1930, pp. 38-39.)

**Paradoxes of Dyslexia.**

The field of dyslexia is full of puzzles and paradoxes. One of the greatest of these is that sometimes – perhaps one can say many times – the student who appears most dumb in the early years of schooling can be among the most capable and successful later on in the world of work – especially when the work is creative and innovative – involving the ability to ponder, think deeply and to see patterns that others do not see.

As one highly successful dyslexic pointed out, it is not hard for a dyslexic to think "out of the box" because, as he says, "they have never been in the box." In contrast, those who could always do quickly exactly what the teacher wanted (getting top grades) can find it very hard – if not impossible – to have a really new thought or to deal successfully with a really new problem or novel situation. They find it easy to retain old knowledge, but they may find it nearly impossible to create new knowledge.

**The Dyslexic Advantage.**

Over the years, I have come to see that one of the most important jobs for dyslexics is to see what others do not see or cannot see – as well as introducing novel ideas that help to avoid the problems of "group think." Diverse brains generating knowledge and perceptions that ordinary brains would never produce.

In recent years, dyslexia is coming to be seen, remarkably, as a significant advantage in an increasing number of fields – often linked to success in design innovation, entrepreneurial business and scientific discovery.

For example, one of the founders of the modern study of molecular biology was dyslexic and described how he used his powerful visual imagination to see new patterns and develop fundamental insights into the links between the genetic code and the immune system (12 years ahead of all others in the field). Later, a different scientist proved experimentally that he was right and received a Nobel Prize.

The US National Science Foundation has been funding a Harvard-Smithsonian study of when and where dyslexia may be an advantage in doing science, especially within astrophysics. In the field of computer graphics and computer simulation, dyslexic artists and technologists are often leading innovators.

A world famous professor of palaeontology tries to teach his graduate students how to think like a dyslexic so they can see patterns invisible to others, long thought impossible. The rest is "just memorization," he says, without innovation or significant discovery.

In recent years researchers have been discovering patterns in neurological structures that help to explain why many dyslexics are so good with high level thinking even though they have so much trouble with low level thinking in their early schooling. (See Drs. Brock and Fernette Eide, *The Dyslexic Advantage*, 2011.)

For example, dyslexics are often highly proficient in big picture and forward-looking thinking – seeing how complex things interact with each other, how a story line will develop, seeing the full potential in a new technology before others, seeing major business opportunities – when everyone else is terrified of coming changes – often seeing patterns that others do not see.

**Personal Discoveries.**

In my early schooling, mostly in a rural state school system, I had learned to read very poorly and very late and had great difficulties with most primary school subjects. This was a puzzle to my teachers and a worry to my otherwise supportive parents.

Even in this comparatively undemanding rural school system, I could barely keep up. I could learn almost nothing by rote. I could not memorize. I could not retain exact texts or numbers. I had to have time to ponder and think. I had to understand. I needed to know the story. I had to find a way to visualize the information. Then, I would never forget.

I knew nothing of my own dyslexia at the time. I was not diagnosed until decades later – at the age of 41. But I did know that there were many things that I could not do – that were quite easy for my classmates. Gradually, in the last years before college, the increasingly high level content began to change what was wanted and what I could produce. Gradually, everything was transformed. The higher level curriculum began to play to my strengths rather than my weaknesses.

Before, I had trouble with arithmetic and "math facts," but in time I came to love geometry, log tables and the slide rule – and eventually got good grades in a course on the philosophy and history of mathematics that I was required to take in college. I had trouble with foreign languages, but loved linguistics and the history of language. I still had lots of trouble with spelling and my slow, faltering reading – but I began to see that I seemed to have a special knack for following logical arguments, complex story lines and higher level conceptual thinking in science and technology.

Gradually, strangely, by my final year before college, I felt that I was getting more out of the readings than many of my classmates. I can still recall, in some detail, almost all of the readings we did during that year.

I went to a small liberal arts college which proved to be the right place, on the whole, for the further growth of these new found capabilities. Remarkably, my major studies were English Literature and Philosophy (so many books to be read and understood) and I later did graduate work in International Relations. I found that I could do high level work – but I had to be careful because I could easily be overwhelmed by large volumes of work.

**School Weaknesses, Work Strengths.**

After graduate school and military service, I was employed by several consulting and engineering companies where I worked in early computer information systems, studies of the effectiveness of certain medical services, developing national energy policy and international trade (participating in one trade mission to four Asian countries and then leading another mission). Eventually, I was the number two manager for a five-year renewable energy development and training program for engineers in Egypt, funded by the US Agency for International Development.

Throughout these work experiences, I found ways around my weaknesses and ways to exploit my talents. I learned to never mention a number unless I had it printed in front of me. I had little technical training, but – usually working with engineers, economists or computer programmers – I found I could easily understand the technical concepts and technical projects at a certain level. Others could be relied on for the data and details. I could write about the projects, explain them, plan them and, eventually, manage them.

**Family Patterns.**

However, I didn't really begin to understand the common difficulties and the common patterns of talent among dyslexics until our own two sons started having problems in their early years of primary school.

The idea that they were going to go through what I had gone through – this was a great emotional shock for me. Suddenly, I realized that I had to understand this thing that had been running my life – and, in part, the life of my dyslexic artist father as well as other family members, more or less.

So I had myself tested for dyslexia. I attended dyslexia conferences and started the research that eventually became the book, *In The Mind's Eye*. I had learned that almost all the professionals in the field wanted mainly to fix reading problems. But that they mostly ignored the special talents that many dyslexics have. Coming from a family of visual-thinking artists and engineers – many with dyslexia or related problems and talents – I realized that there was more to the story than just reading problems.

My research and book focused on these talents as no other book had done before – the neurological foundations, the case studies and profiles of famous people and the growing role of new computer graphic information visualization technologies. As I did my research, I could see the world of technology was changing in fundamental ways – almost all in favour of the dyslexics and their distinctive talents – while, of course, most conventional educators and institutions were then, and still are, blind to these changes.

I was shocked to suddenly realize that, in most cases, the major technological changes unfolding today required skills and talents that seem to come easily to most dyslexics (information visualization) – while the things dyslexics had most difficulty with (rapid reading and spelling) were becoming less and less important in the workplace. Few experts understand the inevitable consequences of this trend.

I suspect that the strong focus on the talents of dyslexics is the reason that the book is still very much alive today – and still regarded as radical new thinking – over twenty years since it was first published in 1991. Even the university research librarians liked it. It was selected as one of the "best of the best" for the year by the American Library Association (one of only 13 books in their broad psychology, psychiatry and neuroscience category).

**Visual Thinkers, Visual Technologies.**

Over the years, I have been invited to give talks and workshops for scientific, medical, art, design, computer and business groups in the U.S. and overseas, including groups in Australia, New Zealand, Canada, Hong Kong, Taiwan and twelve European countries.

I am now working on a third book, this one dealing with high level creativity and brain diversity – including dyslexia and Asperger's syndrome among other alternative modes of learning and thinking – focusing on individuals and families, including one British family with many visual thinkers, many dyslexics and four Nobel Prize winners.

Attitudes toward the special talents of dyslexics have been changing, but very, very slowly. Gradually, non-dyslexics are beginning to see why it is important to have dyslexics involved in their start up businesses or their scientific research.

However, no one could be more surprised than I am with the wide and continuing interest in my books and articles and the ideas they contain. As I started my book research long ago, it was more than a small comfort to me to know that Winston Churchill, for all his major achievements as a leader in time of crisis, had also, once, been at the bottom of the class, feeling "completely outclassed and left behind at the beginning of the race."

For further information read:

**The Dyslexia Advantage** by Drs Brock and Fernette Eide, Published by Hay House UK Ltd.

**In The Mind's Eye** by Thomas West. Published by Prometheus Books

Go to:

**B.D.A. new technology Committee** – provides information and reviews on assistive technology

**www.bdatech.org**

## c. Personal experience: achieving success.
### Jon Adams.

I have never knowingly been ashamed of being dyslexic as it brings its own gifts with it. I unfortunately can't say the same of my time at school where I was 'handled' roughly. It was the early seventies and although I had a 'lust for learning' my writing and spelling let me down, especially in my last year of primary school where I could not hide anymore. A year of constant 'teacher' abuse, being called 'stupid' when I couldn't write, or swot if I 'spoke', led to lasting low self-belief. This was cemented by the tearing up of a picture because I spelt my name wrong.

As an adult I found out why, after 40 years of self imposed exile, I could not perform in the way they expected of me. I did go to University although not for art, which had been my dream since I was 6, but for geology. I seemed to be good at finding things. After this, I became a book illustrator, finding a niche market in 'cutaways.' Due to my dyslexia I could 'visualise in 3D'. My son was diagnosed at school and soon after I was too. Finally realising it wasn't my fault, I often succumbed to depression. Then I realised I had a choice, it wasn't up to others to accept me, it was up to me to accept myself.

I felt very strongly that attitudes to dyslexia were quite wrong; too much emphasis on the 'cant's' and not enough on the 'can'. At school I acquiesced, becoming 'the worthless person' I was told I would always be. Having always felt this was untrue I wanted to prove them wrong. Gone was the worry I would make a fool of myself, and driven by a 'concern' that a dyslexic child in these days shouldn't go through what I did, I pushed forward. Up till then I had drawn other people's pictures; I now had a desire to create for me, a mix of Asperger's literalism and dyslexic experience used intuitively, those things you 'just could not make up.' Seen in a different light, I started receiving grants and later, after a residency, I was kept on by the Local University where I still work now.

In the last few years I have been successfully working on projects within the Cultural Olympiad. My 'Book Flags' public arts project, whilst open to all references 'dyslexia' at its core. It's been presented during Open Weekends, during a torch relay and has been awarded two Inspire Marks but most importantly it has found its way into many schools. Then there's 'Look About', a two year commissioned mapping and collecting project that plays to my dyslexia and aspergers gifts, recently recognised and receiving Cultural Olympiad branding. I am however very proud to have been awarded a fellowship to the Royal Society for the Arts, something very unforeseen by that child, who used to sit head down at his desk. Although I don't regard Dyslexia as a disability, people's attitudes can be. The depressions caused by bullying are haunting, but anything may be possible if you play to your strengths and then persist.

Recently I donated some wood to the 'Boat Project' an arts project creating a sailing boat out of donations and preserving their stories. It was a piece of beech from a cupboard acquired during my old school's refurbishment. It was present in the room while I was abused and I draw a deep satisfaction that it has now rather ironically become part of the 'Tiller and Keel' contributing to a metaphorical cleansing of that time.

# Chapter 8 – Empowerment, campaigning and self-advocacy.

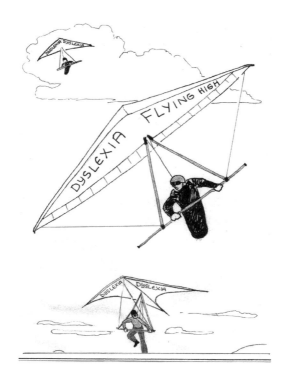

a. The Dyslexic Voice

b. The Dyslexic Individual

c. Mentoring, networks and diversity groups

d. Local Dyslexia Associations

e. Dyslexia is for life not just for school

f. How to get involved

## a. The dyslexic voice.
### Arran Smith.

Dyslexia is still a misunderstood condition and is often only connected with spelling and writing difficulties. Of course we know that, in fact, dyslexia covers a wide range of difficulties and strengths. This means that every dyslexic is different; that only you fully know your dyslexia. You know your strengths and weaknesses and therefore it is you that can explain and spread the word of what dyslexia means to you. It is this understanding of yourself and your difficulties that can help others. Confident dyslexic individuals who believe in themselves are the key to dyslexia awareness. Hearing about other experiences and successes empowers other dyslexic individuals. I am very aware of my weaknesses when it comes to the written word. However, I look on the positive side of dyslexia, that I am able to think out-of-the-box and innovate. Talking and verbal communication is one of my strongest points, as it is for many dyslexic individuals. We must strive to use this skill to empower other dyslexic people to achieve and be a voice for ourselves and all other dyslexics.

This voice of dyslexia can be expressed in many ways by:

- The dyslexic individuals themselves,
- Networks and diversity groups,
- Local Associations and support groups.

## b. The dyslexic individual themselves.
### Carol Leather.

Dyslexia awareness training and campaigning helps to establish a culture of confidence. It acts as a starting point for discussion so that dyslexic individuals feel valued for their different thinking skills. Self-advocacy is a very important part of this dyslexia awareness.

The more people who speak up about what they are going through and about their achievements, the more people will understand. In the workplace dyslexic adults can have a great deal of impact on attitudes towards those with dyslexia and the support provided for them.

To make a difference in the workplace understanding of dyslexia, individuals should be able to:

- explain dyslexia and how it affects them,
- say what their skills are,
- explain what they need to work well.

While in the last two decades much has been done to raise the awareness of dyslexia in the workplace and most organisations do try to work within the spirit of the legislation, there is still a great deal of work to be done. It can be difficult in awareness training to get the balance right. Often in awareness literature when attempting to explain the wide ranging effects of dyslexia, the negative aspects of dyslexia outweigh the positives. Furthermore the negative side e.g. weak literacy skills, are much more visible than the positive creative thinking skills and determination. Therefore the most effective way to promote dyslexia is through the individual themselves.

As one person said to me 'It is really important to me that I am seen for as an individual first and not defined by a stereotype of dyslexia. I want to be able to go into my new manager and say this is what I can do – not talk about what I can't.'

It takes confidence and self-knowledge to self-advocate, the main focus of our work at the Independent Dyslexia Consultants Centre is to help people gain this. We are frequently asked 'when and how should I tell people that I am dyslexic?' It is a personal decision that depends on the circumstances, but it is something that needs to be considered carefully, just saying that you are dyslexic is not enough.

It is important to be confident, positive and to focus on the solutions but also to be aware of any constraints of the job. For example; many people have been given software packages that help with reading and spelling only to discover that they are not compatible with the organisational systems on the computer at work. So using them involves much cutting and pasting and a great deal of time. In this case other solutions, such as a proof reader, might be more effective.

Below is a framework that can help when deciding what to say:

## Sam – a Charity worker.

| Skill | Reason | Outcome |
|---|---|---|
| Good visual skills | Different processing skills | I am good at visual memory aids – I use concept maps and colour charts and this helps everyone. |
| Big picture thinker | Different processing skills | I have lots of ideas – I can see solutions quicker than others. |
| Good people skills | Learned that it was easier to get information from people than books. | I can 'read' people – I am good working in a team. |
| Very organised | Working memory overload – It helps me to remember things. | I now write a to do list and colour code it: red – urgent, amber, green — I get a lot done. |

| Problem | Reason | Solution |
|---|---|---|
| Not participating in meetings | Too many words to process at once | Being well prepared – know the agenda and use a dictaphone or colleague for note-taking |
| Taking too long to produce written work | Poor literacy skills and so I double check | I plan more – and when it is essential to be accurate I ask for it to be proof read |
| Don't know where to start when writing a report | Big picture thinker! | I do a quick draft and talk it through with my colleague to check I am on track |
| Being distracted in a noisy office | Memory overload | I come in early to get organised and get the tricky things done when it's quiet |

Sam said that this process not only helped him talk about being dyslexic but it greatly helped him think through how it affected him in many ways. He also said that he had the confidence to find a compromise when he and his manager had totally different ways of doing things. His manager agreed and also said that she felt she had a much better understanding of Sam, his skills and dyslexia!

## c. Mentoring, networks or diversity groups.
### Carol Leather.

Mentoring and network or diversity groups can provide advice and give people the confidence to ask for what they need in the context of their job. They can seek advice from others who may have had similar experiences, e.g. how best to handle promotion or the appraisal system. These networks also provide an organisational forum to promote good practice and the skills and abilities of dyslexic people. They are most effective when there is a focus on success as well as problems.

> The British Dyslexia Association will support dyslexic individuals (and non-dyslexics!) who wish to set up a mentoring group or network for dyslexic adults in the work place. Please see **www.bdadyslexia.org.uk** or call 0845-251-9003 for further information.

## d. Local Dyslexia Associations.
### Chris Hossack.

Local Dyslexia Associations are an important force in the creation of a dyslexia friendly society. They create a local community for those effected by dyslexia (directly or indirectly) to meet, learn, gain support and campaign.

The British Dyslexia Association (B.D.A.) has over 60 Local Dyslexia Associations (L.D.A.'s) covering most of England, Wales and Northern Ireland. Each has their own charity status and they are mostly run by volunteers who are often dyslexic themselves or a parent of a dyslexic child.

The Local Dyslexia Associations provide help and support for dyslexic adults, children and their families. The services offered depend on the L.D.A. but can include: events, assessment and tutoring services, workshops and coping strategy training. Furthermore, most L.D.A.s have a helpline to signpost to local services and give advice.

It is this local knowledge which is the real strength of L.D.A.s. It means they can affect real change in their local areas. Many local associations have campaigned long and hard to have dyslexia recognised by their education authorities and now plan to establish the ethos of Dyslexia Friendly Schools (DFS) throughout the whole of the teaching community. L.D.A.s also provide the B.D.A. with important information from their area to inform responses to government consultations on national policy.

If you are interested in meeting people striving to make the world dyslexia friendly and join them in helping change and support your local community then L.D.A.s are for you!

> For information on your local dyslexia association or for advice on setting one up near you visit **www.bdadyslexia.org** or call 0845-251-9003

## e. Dyslexia is for life not just school.
### Trevor Hobbs.

The B.D.A. and the local dyslexia associations have worked exceedingly hard over the past four decades to educate the educational establishment as to what dyslexia is and how they could improve the outcome for thousands of pupils by making variations to the way they teach children. It has been a slow, hard battle that is now showing positive results in later life. Thanks to teachers who knew that a child was bright, but had a problem learning, more dyslexics are going on in life to achieve their potential.

In the last decade the focus on dyslexia beyond school and throughout life has grown. The dyslexia movement had to start with children, parents and teachers then as they grew up it has moved on to include employment, adult social life and even retirement years. It is a work in progress.

Having run a dyslexic adult helpline in South London for about fifteen years, I have listened to many accounts of how dyslexia has affected people in their day to day lives. Some stories have been very distressing. It is often due to the lack of understanding by the general population, many of whom still think dyslexia is a problem children have only in school, while others think it means the person is illiterate.

For example, there was the very successful small businessman who relied totally on this wife to undertake all the paperwork. He was the salesman with all the chat, but never talked about his dyslexia. Sadly, she died very suddenly; he lost his wife and his writing hand both at the same time. He feared what the community would think or say if they discovered that he was dyslexic, so in the end he sold the business rather than admit his dyslexia.

Another example is the elderly gentleman in residential care who would throw newspapers and books at people whenever he was given one to read. It was a young care worker who suggested that the gentleman was probably dyslexic as he himself, the carer, was. Both now sit happily and watch the news on the television and the rest of the staff no longer embarrass the old chap by asking him if he would like to read a newspaper every day.

As a nation we still have a long way to go before we reach a dyslexia friendly society. Much needs to be done to make people aware in all areas of life, the community, health and social services and not just education. One of the key areas that needs expertise and some funding is career advice for dyslexics. So many of the callers I try to help are young people who have ended up in the wrong career or with the wrong type of employer and often in the wrong environment. I have had the disability act quoted to me many times by callers who think work is an extension of school life. Getting through school with extra time for study and exams is a great help but these adjustments are often not enough in a work environment.

In reality work is a place that pays by results and employers cannot afford to employ people unable to achieve the required standard, particularly in present day circumstances. Noisy and disorganised workplaces are not easy for most dyslexics but it must be coped with. Many dyslexic people do work well under stress but it must be manageable stress, which means you may not be able to see light at the end of the tunnel but you know there is light to come.

There is also much more emphasis on qualifications. Many dyslexic students have been pressured to go to university when college or apprenticeships and working their way up the company ladder may have been better. Even then it is possible they may reach a point where the job requires a degree. Pleased to be offered promotion the dyslexic person takes on the challenge on the understanding that all they have to do is a normal day's work then go home to study a correspondence course that will lead to the required qualification.

This is likely to be a disaster, the tiredness from the day job and the pressure to complete course work on time can be overwhelming and leaves the dyslexic person miserable. In this case, perhaps the dyslexic would have been better off being grateful for the offer but staying at the level they were comfortable with even if it meant a bit less salary.

We as dyslexics must learn to understand and manage ourselves better. We need to spend time really researching the types of employment that truly fits our individual abilities, lifestyles and ambitions, not what pays the biggest salary or what is the popular career choice this year. Life is hard enough without making it harder through making the wrong career choice. Having to change employers is stressful for everyone but can be a great deal harder for dyslexic people as you have to start all over again telling people that you are dyslexic. However we shouldn't be fearful of change, it can provide the opportunity for people to move into a role or career that suits them better.

A problem that I have seen recently is when a company has been taken over and nobody in new management has been told about the dyslexic employee. Performance and competency issues arise quickly which leads to a loss of confidence and ultimately their job. My advice in this situation is that it is the dyslexic's responsibility to discuss any issues with the new employer – tell them at the start while you have the opportunity to show them what you can do – don't wait till you are snowed under with work and facing the exit only door. Also do not expect them to know what to do, they are not the experts, you are!

I also suggest that people think carefully when applying for jobs and not write dyslexia across every application form because many HR departments still lack a basic understanding of dyslexia. The purpose of an application form is to evaluate if a person has the strengths required to do the job, so present your strengths and sort out your weaker points at a later stage. After being offered a position or at the time of a medical examination can be the best time to disclose your dyslexia if you wish; then talk positively about your dyslexia while just slipping in your limitations.

There is now a great deal of help and advice on a vast array of computer interfaces about employment prospects and work experiences available now. However we also need to remove the stigma that is still associated with being dyslexic by continuing to spread the positive aspects far and wide.

## f. How to get involved.
### Dr. Kate Saunders.

Over the past 40 years, individuals who felt passionately about improving the situation for dyslexic individuals have worked together to move things forward.

Much has been achieved. There is a public awareness of dyslexia and the rights of dyslexic individuals are enshrined in law (eg. the Equality Act 2012). Dyslexic children are helped because we know how to teach dyslexics the way they learn and the importance of early identification (not just for the individual, but as a cost-effective government strategy).

Dyslexic individuals are eligible for access arrangements and support in education and the workplace that they deserve.

However, there is a lack of consistency in the services and support available for dyslexic individuals. It is a patchy picture of delivery and all too often, only the best informed (who can assert their rights) manage to access the services that should be routinely available to all. There are also huge holes in provision: there is no mechanism for an adult who isn't in higher education to receive funding for an assessment and unemployed dyslexic individuals are in a provision desert.

Far too many dyslexic individuals still experience serious barriers to their potential. It is not an unusual story for dyslexic children frustrated in school to end up excluded and then in dead-end jobs or worse in youth offending and prison services (research suggests the 52% of the prison population has literacy difficulties including dyslexia[1]). This is a field where, above all, dedicated individuals make a positive difference.

---

1    The Dyslexia Institute (2005) The Incidence of hidden disabilities in the prison population.

The future for dyslexic adults, their children and future generations, depends upon people who care about these issues getting involved. Everyone has something to offer that can combine with the efforts of others to make a real difference. Together we can make a real difference. It's all worthwhile.

- Support current dyslexia campaigns (see **www.bdadyslexia.org.uk**)

- Spread the word about dyslexia: talk about your experience, join in the activities in the annual Dyslexia Awareness Week (October) and help reduce stigma

- Join your local dyslexia association and the B.D.A.

- Attend conferences and talks organised: to learn more about dyslexia and meet other interested people

- Donate or fundraise to support the work of the B.D.A.: run a marathon, sky dive or have a coffee morning or donate to our raffles.

- Reward achievement: nominate someone for a B.D.A. annual award

- Be a positive role model: change perceptions by talking and writing about your experiences and strengths. Seize and create opportunities to help build a dyslexia friendly society.

# Chapter 9 – Resources Directory.

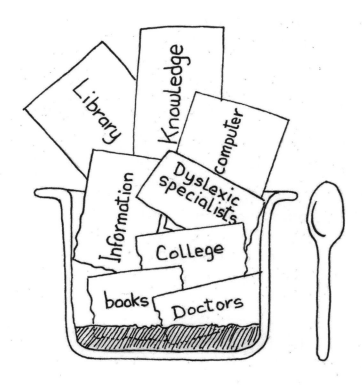

## Advice & Support.

**B.D.A. helpline** – National helpline providing information and advice **(Monday to Friday** 10:00am – I 4:00pm open late on Tuesday and Wednesday from 5:00pm – 7:00pm.) 0845-251-9002

**British Dyslexia Association Website** – Information and advice on dyslexia **www.bdadyslexia.org.uk**

**Citizens Advice Bureau** – advice to everyone on their rights and responsibilities, especially helpful with Local Authority issues **www.citizensadvice.org.uk**

**Local Dyslexia Associations** – Associations throughout the country offering advice and support **www.bdadyslexia.org.uk/membership/ directories/lda-directory.html**

## Art.

**Arts Dyslexia Trust** – provides information about training and careers and promotes dyslexic artists **www.Artsdyslexiatrust.org**.

**Dyslexia, Music and the Performing Arts** – Edited by Sally Daunt. Published by the British Dyslexia Association

## Assessments.

**Access to work** – Arrange work place assessments Tel: 02920 423291 **www.directgov.uk/accesstowork**

**British Psychology Society** – Find local educational psychologists Tel: 0116-254-9568 **www.bps.org.uk**

**British Dyslexia Association** – provides lists of local specialists teachers
Tel:0845-251-9003 **www.bdadyslexia.org.uk**

**Dyslexia Action** – Assessment centres across the country
Tel: 01784-222-300 **www.dyslexiaaction.org.uk**

**Helen Arkell Dyslexia Centre** – Assessment Centre and can provide list of local specialist teachers
Tel: 01252-792-400 **www.arkellcentre.org.uk**

**PATOSS** – Can provide list of local specialist teacher
Tel: 01386-712-650 **www.patoss-dyslexia.org**

**Working with Dyslexia** – information on assessments including videos of people talking about their assessment experience **www.workingwithdyslexia.com**.

## Assistive Technology.

**Ability Net** – Assistive It Support
Tel: 0800-269-545 **www.abilitynet.org.uk**

**B.D.A. New Technology Committee** – provides information and reviews on assistive technology **www.bdatech.org**

**Calibre** – audio books for loan
Tel: 01296-432-339 **www.calibre.co.uk**

**ClaroRead** – text to speech software
**www.clarosoftware.com**

**Crossbow education** – visual stress and dyslexia support supplies
Tel: 0845-269-7272 **www.crossboweducation.com**

**Dragon NaturallySpeaking** – Speech to text software
**www.nuance.com/dragon**

**Dyslexia and Useful technology** – Edited E.A Draffen
Published by the British Dyslexia Association

**Emptech** – provides information on assistive technology
**www.emptech.info/index.php**

**Google Calendar** – Electronic calendars
**www.google.com/calendar**

**ImTranslator** – online text to speech in other languages
**www.imtranslator.com**

**Insyst** – Assistive IT supplier
Tel: 0800-018-0045 **www.dyslexic.com**

**Listening books** – audio books for loan
Tel: 020-7407-9417 **www.listening-books.org.uk**

**Live Scribe** – Note taking software
**www.livescribe.com/uk/**

**Microlink PC** – Assistive IT supplier
Tel: 0808-1180-487 **www.microlinkpc.co.uk**

**Recom** – reconditioned computers charity
Tel:0121-663-0335 **www.recom.org.uk**

**Texthelp Read and Write Gold** – Text to speech software
**www.texthelp.com/UK**

**Word Shark** – programme to help with learning spelling
**www.wordshark.co.uk** (also see Phone apps)

## Attention deficit disorder.

**AADD-UK** – provides information and support for adults with Attention Deficit (Hyperactivity) Disorder
**www.aadduk.org**

**ADD-friendly ways to Organise your Life** – book by Judith Kolberg and Kathleen Nadeau. Publishe by Routledge.

**Development Adult neuro-Diversity Association** – Information and support for idividuals with Dyspraxia, ADHD, aspergers and other related conditions
**www.danda.org.uk**

**Delivered from Distraction** – by Edward Hallowell and Luke Ratey. Published by Ballanteine

## Books.

**The Dyslexia Advantage** – by Drs Brock and Fernette Eide. Published by Hay House UK Ltd.

**Dyslexia – A Beginner's Guide** – by Nicola Brunswick. Published by Oneworld

**Dyslexia and Co-occuring difficulties** – Edited by Professor John Stein published by British Dyslexia Association

**Dyslexia in the Workplace** – by Margaret Malpas. Published by British Dyslexia Assocaiton

**Dyslexia: How to Survive and Succeed at Work** – By Sylvia Moody. Published by Random House (Vermilion).

**The Gift of Dyslexia** – By Ronald D Davis. Published by Souvenir Press Ltd

**In The Mind's Eye** – by Thomas West.
Published by Prometheus Books

**Making Dyslexia Work for You** – by Vicki Goodwin
and Bonita Thomson. Published by Routledge

**The Principles of Success** – by Professor
Patrick Jordan. Published by WWPC Ltd.

**That's the way I think: dyslexia and dyspraxia explained**
– by David Grant. Published by David Fulton Books.

**Supporting Dyslexic Adults in Higher
education and Employment** – edited by Nicola
Brunswick. Published by Wiley-Blackwell

## Careers.

**Brian Hagan** – author of Choosing a Career in
this book can provide dyslexia specific advice &
training services – **bhdyslexia@yahoo.co.uk**

**Disability Job Site** – provides guidance and job searches
**www.disabilityjobsite.co.uk**

**Employ-ability** – Careers advice for disabled graduates
**www.employ-ability.org.uk**

**The National Careers Service** – national careers information
and advice **nationalcareersservice.direct.gov.uk**

**Palgrave Study Skills** – provides information and suggest
resources forpersonal development and career choice
**www.palgrave.com/skills4study/pdp/useful/index.asp**

## Discrimination information.

**British Dyslexia Association website** – information about disability discrimination and your rights
**http://www.bdadyslexia.org.uk/about-dyslexia/adults-and-business/disability-discrimination-act-.html**

**The Disability Law Service** (provides free legal advice to disabled people and representation where appropriate.)
Tel: 020-7791-9800 Web: **http://www.dls.org.uk**

**HE discrimination Complaints** – Independent Adjudicator of HE (to be contacted after going through university channels)
0118-959-9813

**Business Disability Forum** – organisation focussed on disability as it affects business.
Tel: 020-7403-3020 Web: **www.efd.org.uk**

**Equality Human Rights Commission** – information on what the Equality Act 2010 means **http://www.equalityhumanrights.com/advice-and-guidance/new-equality-act-guidance/**

**RADAR** is able to give advice on the Act.
Tel: 020-7250-3222 Web: **http://www.radar.org.uk**

## Disabled Student Allowance.

**Disabled Student Allowance** – Government information on the Disabled Student Allowance **www.direct.gov.uk** (search disabled student allowance in the help box)

**Disabled Student Allowances Quality Assurances** – provides list of centres for DSA tests
**www.dsa-qag.org.uk**

## Driving.

**Driving Standards Agency** – to ask for extra time or a voiceover during your theory test 0300-200-1122 **www.direct.gov.uk**

**DSA app Theory Test for Car Drivers Kit**: – for theory test revision available from iTunes store

**Driving Test Success by Focus Software** – highly recommended by driving instructors experienced in candidates with specific learning difficulties. Available from Amazon.

## Dyspraxia.

**Development Adult Neuro-Diversity Association** – Information and support for individuals with Dyspraxia, ADHD, aspergers and other related conditions **www.danda.org.uk**

**Living with Dyspraxia.** – by Mary Colley. Published by Jessica Kingsley.

## Phone Apps.

**2 Do app** – good interface for creating lists **www.2doapp.com/**

**Quinnscape** – useful for helping you pack and remember to bring things: **www.quinnscape.com/**

**Epic Win** – A game style to do list app **itunes.apple.com/gb/app/epicwin/id372927221?mt=8**

**Evernote** –helps you remember thoughts, ideas and people with text, photos and audio **www.evernote.com**

**Expense manager** – Money organising app for android **play.google.com/store/apps/details?id=com. expensemanager&hl=en**

**Mint money manager** – Money organising for smart phones and computer **www.mint.com/t/012/**

## Screening Tests.

**Spot your potential** – online screening test **www.spot-your-potential.com** or **www.bdadyslexia.org.uk**

**Quick Scan** – from Pico education Systems **www.studyscan.com**

**LADs** – from Lucid Research **www.lucid-research.co.uk**

## Study Skills.

**Inclusive Solutions** – Learning style screening and information **www.outsider.co-uk.com**

**Brain.HE** – information and resources for students including the holist manifesto, social model of disability **www.brainhe.com**

**Super Reading** – Proof Reading courses **www.outsider.co-uk.com/superreading**

## Tutors

**British Dyslexia Association** – can provide lists of local specialists teachers
Tel: 0845-251-9002  **www.bdadyslexia.org.uk**

**Dyslexia Action** – has centres across the country offering tuition
Tel: 01784-222-300 **www.dyslexiaaction.org.uk**

**Helen Arkell Dyslexia Centre** – Can provide list of local specialist teachers
Tel: **01252-792-400 www.arkellcentre.org.uk**

**PATOSS** – Can provide list of local specialist teacher
Tel: 01386-712-650 **www.patoss-dyslexia.org**

**Visual Stress**

**Dyslexia Research Trust** – provides eye tests
**www.dyslexic.org.uk**

**Institute of Colorimetry** – provides information and lists of opticians **www.colorimetryinstitute.org/**